AMERICAN POSSESSIONS

FIGHTING DEMONS IN THE CONTEMPORARY UNITED STATES

SEAN McCLOUD

OXFORD
UNIVERSITY PRESS

OXFORD
UNIVERSITY PRESS

Oxford University Press is a department of the University of Oxford.
It furthers the University's objective of excellence in research, scholarship,
and education by publishing worldwide.

Oxford   New York
Auckland   Cape Town   Dar es Salaam   Hong Kong   Karachi
Kuala Lumpur   Madrid   Melbourne   Mexico City   Nairobi
New Delhi   Shanghai   Taipei   Toronto

With offices in
Argentina   Austria   Brazil   Chile   Czech Republic   France   Greece
Guatemala   Hungary   Italy   Japan   Poland   Portugal   Singapore
South Korea   Switzerland   Thailand   Turkey   Ukraine   Vietnam

Oxford is a registered trade mark of Oxford University Press
in the UK and certain other countries.

Published in the United States of America by
Oxford University Press
198 Madison Avenue, New York, NY 10016

Library of Congress Cataloging-in-Publication Data
McCloud, Sean.
American possessions : fighting demons in the contemporary United States /
Sean McCloud.
p.   cm.
Includes bibliographical references and index.
ISBN 978–0–19–020535–5 (cloth : alk. paper)   1. Demonic possession—United States.
2. Spiritual warfare—United States. I. Title.
BL482.M355 2015
235'.40973—dc23

2014037125

1   3   5   7   9   8   6   4   2

Printed in the United States of America on acid-free paper

This book is dedicated to the ghosts that haunt me,
always out of reach but all too real

CONTENTS

ACKNOWLEDGMENTS

Books are written within moments of history. And history is always both personal and social. The biographical creative fictions and the imposed material conditions with which we make up our lives bleed into our writing, regardless of the subject. One recurring motif in this work deals with repressed (or at least downplayed) history and how it haunts the present. I think of acknowledgments pages as a partial history of a book, a history of the social relationships and (if the author was lucky) institutional support from which the pages that follow were born. I say "partial" because acknowledgments pages are—like the books they appear in—also written within a specific historical moment. It takes time to write a book, and lots of things happen that usually don't get mentioned in an acknowledgment, even if they were crucial in the author's life at the time. Loved ones are born and loved ones die. Friendships begin, friendships end. Interests change and things that once engaged someone may later seem insignificant, while new pursuits stir excitement. A lot happened to me while I worked on this book that no doubt influenced my writing, some of which I am not even conscious of in this moment. I do wonder how these acknowledgments might read differently if I were to write them years from now.

I became indebted to many for their comments, conversations, and kindnesses while writing this book, and I am pleased to thank them here. First, I thank Lynn Abbott-McCloud and Sinead Abbott-McCloud for their support. I mean, geez, I know I couldn't live with me, so I am impressed and pleased that they can. Lynn's mum, Joan Abbott, lived with us and died with us as I was researching this work.

She was always supportive of me and has my sincerest thanks for all her positive encouragement and compliments.

Jason Bivins, Katie Lofton, Amy DeRogatis, Courtney Stromme, Kat Daley-Bailey, Dave McConeghy, Kelly Baker, Ritika Prasad, and Craig Martin read varying portions of the manuscript in progress and provided useful comments as well as kind words. Conversations with Katja Rakow about the contemporary intertwining of American religions, neoliberalism, and therapeutic discourse helped me clarify my thinking on these matters, and she has my gratitude. Thank you to Ann Richelle Naj Feign for acting as a long-distance writing policeman who made regular check-ins on me during my most intense period of writing. I also found much to appreciate in Annie's poems about haunting pasts while I was working on topically related sections of this book. Though I have always had an ambivalent relationship with it, at one point, Facebook proved to be a good place where I could ask questions pertaining to my research and get quick answers (and you thought it was just for posting cat pictures and dinner menus). In addition to Kat, Craig, Kelly, and Katja mentioned earlier, I benefited from the comments of Rich King, Russell McCutcheon, Chip Callahan, Gordon Lynch, Titus Hjelm, Mara Einstein, Matt Hedstrom, Alison Buck, Megan Goodwin, Horacio Castillo, John Modern, Dawn Lewellyn, Josh Paddison, and Ginger Stickney.

During the fall semester of 2012, I had the fortune of being awarded a research leave by my university. During that time I was offered a non-stipendiary research fellowship at Indiana University's Poynter Center for the Study of Ethics and American Institutions. It was in my office at the Poynter Center that the most significant re-visioning of this project took place, and I am grateful to Richard Miller, Stuart Yoak, Ken Pimple, Glenda Murray, Emma Young, Beth Works, Cheryl Cottine, Mary Ulmet, and Na Qin for their hospitality and kindness.

During my Bloomington stay, I benefited from giving several talks. In addition to those named above, I thank Sarah Imhoff, Rita Lichtenberg, and Don Lichtenberg for their thoughts and comments at my September 2012 Poynter Center lecture. Thanks to everyone—especially Monica Florence, Jeremy Rapport, and Mark Graham—for their comments and conversations during my visit and lecture at the College of Wooster in November 2012. Finally, my two paper presentations in late November 2012 at the Chicago American Academy of Religion Meeting made for a nice closing to the small, but immensely useful, "American Possessions Tour" of the Great Lakes region.

I was fortunate to have a kind and thorough editor in Theo Calderara at Oxford University Press. He and his assistant, Marcela Maxfield, did an excellent job. Thanks as well to Claire Weatherhead at Bloomsbury publishing for permission to reprint portions of my article, "Mapping the Spatial Limbos of Spiritual Warfare: Haunted Houses, Defiled Land, and Horrors of History." *Material Religion: The Journal of Objects, Art, and Belief* 9:2 (June 2013). 166–185. That piece is the basis for chapter two of this work.

Thank you to Scott Shellhamer for creating and giving me permission to use the art that appears on the cover of this book. Thanks also go to Dean Nancy Gutierrez and The University of North Carolina at Charlotte's College of Liberal Arts and Sciences for providing funds for Scott's work.

More than any other long-term writing project on which I have worked, this book was accompanied by a continuous soundtrack. In no particular order, I thank Amber Comber Smith, Jason Smith, Mike Toler, Mary Hamner, Mike Bulington, Matt Whitaker, Sinead Abbott-McCloud, Lynn Abbott-McCloud, and Adam Colvin for making music with me during the writing period. I also learned about new music and had a great time revisiting older sounds with Jason Bivins, Leah Drayton, Amber Comber Smith, Daren Hill, Scott Shellhamer, G. Therese Lanz, Annie Feign, Kevin "Burd" Burdeshaw, Jeff Bulington, and Mike Bulington. Music has always been very important to me and I am certain that listening to, sharing, and playing it helped me write (and that's my story, even if I have absolutely no empirical evidence whatsoever to support this claim).

August 2014

AMERICAN POSSESSIONS

INTRODUCTION

AMERICAN RELIGION IN AN ERA
OF POSSESSIONS

In April 2012, ABC's *Nightline* featured a story on three teenage girls who—in addition to their hobbies of shopping and horseback riding, attending musicals and beauty pageants—spent large portions of their time exorcising demons. "We're just normal girls who do something extraordinary for God," said Brynne Larson, the home-schooled leader of the teen exorcists and daughter of demon-hunting evangelical Bob Larson. "There is a war going on every day, being waged against us," Brynne told the *Nightline* journalist. "Satan hates us. We know who the enemy is, we know what he's attacking and we can fight back."[1] The interviews were interlaced with footage of prayers, shouts, laying on of hands, and a few guttural voices as the girls battled unseen demons.

The story wasn't the first on the trio and Bob Larson's self-described "exorcist franchise." In August 2011, the *Daily Mail* (UK) ran one of the initial stories, noting that the girls' accessories included a Bible, holy water, and a cross. *Mail* journalist Jeff Maysh described Brynne as "highly experienced in casting out demons, saving souls, and banishing evil spirits to hell," but also someone "who enjoys styling her hair, shopping and meeting friends at Starbucks." Fellow exorcist Tess Schurkenback, whose Bible was described in the story as a particularly "attractive, red leather-bound" one, detailed the two parts of their exorcism work, noting that, first "you must deal with inner healing, to get rid of traumatic experiences from your childhood and beyond, and secondly, deliverance from demons." "We have found," said Bob Larson, "that our female, teenage exorcists are particularly effective at curing the possessed."[2]

The Arizona trio received more than their fifteen minutes of fame, including television appearances on CNN and ABC, blog items at *Huffington Post* and *Esquire*, and stories in as variant and far-flung periodicals as the German edition of *Glamour* (the writer interviewed the teens at the Scottsdale Fashion Square Mall).[3] By February 2014, a Google search on the term "teen exorcists" returned more than 17,000 results, and one could visit the girls' official website (Teenageexorcists. com) and accompanying Facebook page. Bob Larson and the girls expressed the hope that they would soon star in a reality television show that would follow their demon-fighting exploits.

Media commentary on the teenage exorcists was predictably snarky. The response of *Esquire*'s Charles Pierce to the *Nightline* piece was typical in its accusations of charlatanism, use of the word "cult," and the mockery of both the girls' and their clients' intelligence. Pierce, typically snarky, labeled the girls "Forever 21 medievalists" and said the story read like the *Malleus Maleficarum* if it were written by Judy Blume. Indeed, such commentary mirrored the sort of coverage garnered by religious movements, practices, and ideas unfamiliar to journalists and their social locations since at least the 1950s.[4] Frankly, some skepticism appeared due. The demon deliverances (the evangelical term for exorcisms) cost between $400 and $500 (plus travel expenses), and Bob Larson had more than a bit of P.T. Barnum in him; his activities had, in the past, garnered criticism even from other deliverance ministries.[5] And it was Larson himself who appeared to be driving the coverage, sending out press releases about his teen exorcist training school and actively shopping a reality show. While he and the girls were no doubt dead serious in their demon-busting activities, the blatant self-promotion and evil-spirit exiling fees stirred suspicion among journalists—who have long imagined (wrongly) that "true religion" and capitalism don't mix.

Pierce's reaction—in addition to the coverage on CNN, ABC, and in various print and Internet media outlets—missed the importance of the story, something much larger and diffuse than Brynne, her two BFFs, and her attention-seeking father. If reporters had dug deeper, they might have found that the keywords appearing repeatedly in the teen exorcist coverage—deliverance/exorcism, demons, shopping, therapy, inner healing, curses, reality television, haunted homes—pointed toward some of the most important forces shaping American religion in the early twenty-first century.

ARGUMENTS

Bob Larson and his teenage exorcists grabbed headlines, but they were a sideshow act compared to a theologically related—and much more influential—group of demon-fighting Protestants who call their activities "spiritual warfare." They will be the focus of this book. This loose-knit collection of neo-Pentecostal, charismatic, independent, and denominational evangelicals are part of a thirty-plus-year-old movement whose founders named it the "Third Wave." In *American Possessions,* I argue two primary things. First, I suggest that U.S. religious culture in the twenty-first century is best characterized as one of possessions—of both consumer goods and spirit entities—that is thoroughly saturated with the language of the therapeutic. These three themes—the consumerist, the haunted, and the therapeutic—converge in Third Wave evangelicalism. Second, I argue that the theology of the Third Wave and spiritual warfare both complements and contests contemporary discourses concerning agency, structure, history, and conceptions of the individual—specifically, these ideas as they are conceived within the historical conglomeration of economic, political, and cultural activities and ideologies grouped under the term "neoliberalism."[6]

APPROACHES AND CAVEATS

American Possessions is an interdisciplinary work that most directly fits within the field aptly named by Jason Bivins "American religious studies."[7] While the study of American religions first emerged in Christian seminaries under the name "church history," the field has expanded in the last two decades beyond denominational histories—and indeed beyond the method of history itself—to incorporate a broader range of subjects and approaches. This has not occurred without a good deal of handwringing, and the boundaries marking what subjects, approaches, and theoretical orientations are acceptable are constantly shifting. Putting these academic harangues aside (or, in this case, relegating them to the endnotes), I am struck that much useful and engaging scholarship in American religious studies has been produced in recent years, and my hope is that *American Possessions* complements and converses with some of it.[8]

First, I see this study of Third Wave spiritual warfare as corresponding in some ways with Kathryn Lofton's *Oprah: The Gospel of an Icon*. Lofton's focus was on an ostensibly nonreligious media figure—Oprah Winfrey—and how religion and consumption combined in her celebrity persona, activities, and products. Lofton argues that "the products of Oprah's empire offer a description of religion in modern society." My focus is on an ostensibly religious movement and how its idioms and practices are inextricably linked with the contemporary discourses of consumer capitalism, popular culture, politics, and neoliberalism. Just as Oprah does for Lofton, I suggest that an examination of Third Wave spiritual warfare provides a view of larger trends in contemporary American religion and culture.[9]

The subject of this work is not just Third Wave evangelicalism, but the demons that haunt its imaginary. My sources for conjuring these evil spirits (or at least the words I write about them) are primarily dozens of spiritual warfare handbooks written by prominent Third Wave figures, but also mass-media productions such as documentaries, websites, and television shows. Given my subject and sources, I am heartened and bolstered by recent scholarship exploring what might be called the "darker side" of religious studies. Works such as Jason Bivins' *Religion of Fear* and Kelly Baker's *Gospel According to the Klan* provide useful models for studying the dead serious doom and gloom of American religion.[10] Perhaps even more important, though, is that they demonstrate how sources such as racist pamphlets, Chick Tracts, Klan newspapers, hell house performances, and the anti-occult section of Christian bookstores are just as much "archival material" as the sermons of Puritan minsters, the diaries of Colonial merchants, and the proclamations of American bishops.[11]

Let me also note what I won't be doing. First, I won't be attending to issues of "secularization." This classical sociological model has been debated for decades.[12] Recently, we see scholars such as Charles Taylor declaring the present a secular age of disenchantment and Steve Bruce telling us that God is finally dead.[13] Meanwhile, their detractors declare secularization bunk and point to a world full of people who continue to hold supernatural ideas dear, whether those are about a god, gods, powers, or ghosts.[14] I think that such discussions can be productive, but I am not interested here in examining the Third Wave and its demons as either a vestigial premodern holdout or a fresh new supernaturalist shot across the bow of secularization. In brief, I am influenced by scholars who note that the genesis of the modern "secular" was constituted within certain forms of Protestantism.[15] In more than one way, "secular" only exists through its equally dependent binary, "religion." Rather than debating whether we live in an enchanted or disenchanted era, I agree with the American religious historian John Modern that, "one must recognize the distinction between enchantment and disenchantment as integral to the modern secular imaginary and not as some natural difference between two modes of consciousness."[16]

The second caveat is that this is not a history of the Third Wave, nor an examination of the Christian genealogies of spiritual warfare and conceptions of demons. That work already exists, the former produced by scholars such as René Holvast and Thomas Pratt and journalists such as Bruce Wilson and Rachel Tabachnick.[17] Descriptions of the Third Wave can be found in encyclopedias of evangelicalism and overviews of Christian theology.[18] Other scholars have examined aspects of Third Wave practices under the rubrics of "spiritual warfare," "spiritual mapping," and "neo-Pentecostalism," which are all associated with the movement.[19] My goal in writing *American Possessions* is not to repeat information that others have already gathered and produced, but rather to answer questions that American religion scholars have yet to pose: What kinds of "work" does spiritual warfare do for

Third Wave practitioners? What does this demon-haunted evangelical landscape tell us about contemporary American religion and culture?

To answer these questions, of course, does require some historical and sociological contextualization. In the remainder of this introduction, I first give a very brief history and overview of the Third Wave and its practices, and next expand upon the three characterizations—the consumerist, the haunted, and the therapeutic—that partly describes the contemporary period.

THE THIRD WAVE

The "Third Wave" is a term coined by former Fuller Theological Seminary professor C. Peter Wagner in several articles and books he wrote in the 1980s. These writings grew out of a course he taught with John Wimber, "Signs, Wonders, and Church Growth." The name described what he and some of his colleagues viewed as a new evangelical movement of the Holy Spirit—the latest in an historical succession with two previous "waves," the birth of Pentecostalism at the turn of the twentieth century and the charismatic movement of the 1960s and early 1970s. Though this self-described Third Wave of American evangelicalism has received only minor attention from religious studies scholars, its influence can be seen in as variant examples as the New Apostolic Reformation's 2011 prayer conference featuring former Republican presidential candidate Rick Perry; televangelist Pat Robertson's 2010 comment that the Haitian earthquake was caused by a pact the country's founders made with Satan; former Alaskan governor Sarah Palin's videotaped deliverance prayer by an African exorcist; and evangelical missionary strategies in Asia, the Caribbean, Africa, and Latin America.[20] The term "Third Wave" may not be known to everyone, and Wagner is far from a household name, but the phenomenon is likely to have registered, however fleetingly, on many people's radar screens.

There are undoubtedly several reasons for the paucity of scholarly attention to the Third Wave and spiritual warfare, including the social distance between most academics and those who participate in Third Wave activities (making them nearly invisible to some) and the discomfort the movement causes for various evangelical scholars, who view them as the unrefined cousins they pretend they're not related to (some wish they were *more* invisible). But another reason is that the movement is diffuse and loose, made up of groups and individuals connected primarily by practices and theologies of spiritual warfare. Leaders in the movement generally avoid the "Third Wave" moniker, preferring to reference specific movements (such as the New Apostolic Reformation) or practices (such as strategic-level spiritual warfare) that fall under the Third Wave umbrella. Some practitioners know little of the Third Wave's history and figures, but are still influenced by its idioms.[21] But don't be mistaken, the Third Wave consists of multiple institutional structures that are well funded and expansive in their geographical, cultural, and political reach. These include (or have included) the U.S. Strategic Prayer Network, the Sentinel Group, the New Apostolic Reformation, Spiritual Warfare Network, Justice at the Gate, Christian Harvest International, the U.S. Prayer Center, Glory of Zion International Ministries, Generals International, Global Harvest Ministries, and the Wagner Leadership Institute. Prominent members have served on boards of organizations such as the charismatic group Women's Aglow, and well-known figures have staked their claim as fellow travelers. The evangelical pollster George Barna, for example, appeared in promotional films for the Sentinel Group's "Transformations" series, and the scandal-plagued pastor Ted Haggard, former head of the largest evangelical umbrella organization in the United States, provided a blurb for a Third Wave author's book.[22] This is no small and uninfluential group.

Most of the movement's founders and major figures are based in the United States, including Peter Wagner, Cindy Jacobs, George Otis Jr., Ed Murphy, Eddie and Alice Smith, Rebecca Greenwood, and Chuck Pierce. Some of the Third Wave's largest publishers and organizational structures are based in Southern California, reflecting the connection between the region and the larger conservative evangelical movement, a history that has been recently traced by the historian Darren Dochuk.[23] At the same time, interviews with current and former participants suggest that the movement is well represented throughout the United States, with members performing spiritual mapping in rural Michigan towns, publishing books in Florida, delivering individuals and their possessions from demons in North Carolina, performing intercessory prayers on behalf of others in Maine and Texas, staking the land for Jesus in suburban Colorado, and taking special classes on spiritual warfare in small-town Indiana churches. Third Wave evangelicalism is also deeply involved in and largely dependent upon mission fields outside the United States, in countries such as Guatemala, Nicaragua, Singapore, Papua New Guinea, and other locations in Africa, South America, and Southern and East Asia.[24] The "dependence" suggested here lies in the importance of international missions for fantastical first-person supernatural tales and the development of Third Wave demonology, which views all non-evangelical religions as satanic because they are believed to promote "contact with, worship of, homage to, and even use of spirit beings other than the one true God."[25] In other words, all non-evangelical religious figures (ranging from the Buddha to the Virgin Mary) and religious objects and sites (from Native American jewelry and African statuary to Shinto temples and Masonic lodges) are viewed as either actual demons or the abodes of demonic presence.

The "spiritual" and "material/natural" worlds are tightly intertwined in Third Wave theology. "The natural," writes the Guatemalan pastor, one-time presidential candidate, and Spiritual Warfare Network area coordinator Harold Caballeros, "is only a reflection of the spiritual, and a connection between them always exists."[26] The majority of Third Wave evangelicals are Pentecostals, charismatics, and neo-Pentecostals who hold to a belief in divinely imparted "gifts of the spirit," citing—among other passages—I Corinthians 12 and 14 and Acts 2: 1–4 to suggest that Christians have the divine ability to heal, prophesize, speak in tongues, and cast out demons. Because of this, activities and experiences such as glossolalia and dancing in the spirit provide physical "proof" of the realities of the spirit world. Physical experience as proof is so crucial that some Third Wave theologians suggest that biblical interpretation must be evaluated and judged through experience. The deliverance counselor Ed Murphy, for example, writes that "correct biblical interpretation is that interpretation which is most consistent with experience," and that "theology which is contradicted by experience, or at least brought into question, is theology that needs to be reexamined."[27]

One of the clusters of experiences given significant weight in Third Wave theology is that of encounters with demons on earth. Pentecostals, charismatics, Roman Catholics, and several other types of Christians have long believed in demons and have engaged in exorcisms to expel them. But the birth of the demon-fighting Third Wave movement in the late 1980s and early 1990s appears especially noteworthy when one considers that the period roughly corresponds to, first, the appearance of "satanic panics" in rural areas and small towns and the resulting mass media coverage, and, second, the expansion of the New Christian Right and its (sometimes literal) demonization of liberal and left-wing politics.[28] As will be seen in the first chapter, Third Wave writers not only continue to claim—against all evidence—the existence of satanic cults that commit ritual abuse and murder, but they very literally demonize the Democratic party, in effect resembling a religious arm of the contemporary American far right.

SPIRITUAL WARFARE HANDBOOKS AND THEIR DEMONS

Spiritual warfare is the conflict between the Kingdom of Light and the kingdom of darkness, or Satan's kingdom. The two kingdoms are competing for the souls and spirits of the people who inhabit the earth. This results in an ongoing battle involving two realms, the visible realm and the invisible realm. The spiritual battle that takes place in the heavenlies, in the invisible realm, is initiated in the hearts of people and has its final effect here on earth, in the visible realm.[29]

The primary (though not sole) sources I examine in *American Possessions* are the handbooks—variously called by their authors "training manuals," "how-to" tomes, and "practical guides"—that teach practitioners how to conduct spiritual warfare against Satan and his soldiers, who are busy tormenting and infesting individuals (ground-level warfare), movements (occult-level warfare), and entire cities, regions, and nation-states (strategic-level warfare).[30]

A significant part of the Third Wave evangelical imaginary is an apocalyptic reading of history, at the heart of which is the idea that we are currently living in the end times. In these final days, Satan has amassed an army of evil spirits that he is using to attack and demonize humans in an effort to win souls for hell. To properly combat the Devil and his minions, Third Wave practitioners have produced numerous spiritual warfare handbooks. These "how-to" battle manuals teach three primary methods for interceding in the supernatural war being waged on earth. First are deliverance rituals, uniquely evangelical Protestant forms of exorcism—distinct from those long practiced by the Catholic Church—designed to banish demons from individuals' bodies. Second is a genre concerned with "spiritual housecleaning" that features ritual practices focused on personal objects, homes, and property believed to be demon-inhabited. Third is the practice of "spiritual mapping," a Third Wave version of geomancy that discerns where and why demons control spaces and places, ranging from houses and neighborhoods to entire countries. Spiritual mapping entails researching a place to understand its history in relation to evangelicalism and other religions and praying to God for divine guidance in seeing "spiritual realities" missing in the historical record.

Demons play *the* crucial role in the Third Wave imaginary. Third Wave practitioners' interests in demons are, to quote the historian Walter Stephens' description of medieval European demonologists' concerns, "inseparable from their theological concerns, not an eccentric sideline."[31] As spiritual beings who regularly take on a physical presence in the material world, demons do several kinds of work in the Third Wave imaginary. First, they provide a very material and spatially located form of theodicy, explaining why certain places, objects, and people have been—and continue to be—witness to tragedy and sin. Events and phenomena as variant as plane disappearances in the Bermuda Triangle, the 2010 Haitian Earthquake, haunted houses, generational alcoholism in families, and national financial crises are all explained via some combination of human sins and demonic activities. Second, demons are the focal point of attention and attack in spiritual warfare. Because Satan and his evil spirits stand between the individual and her salvation through Jesus Christ, expelling demons from people, objects, and places is the goal of spiritual warfare practices. Third, and most broadly, in asserting the reality and even physical presence of demons, one simultaneously asserts the reality of the entire Third Wave theology of God, Satan, and the spiritual world. To put it simply, without the demonic there would be no Third Wave spiritual warfare.

Third Wave theologies—filled as they are with images of demons, idioms of warfare, and assurances of an imminent end time—may seem far removed from what many religion scholars view as the "American mainline" of religious practice. Perhaps it doesn't look like an Episcopalian church service or Methodist coffee hour, but the movement registers some of the most prescient themes in contemporary American religion.

The Consumerist, the Haunted, and the Therapeutic: Themes in Contemporary American Religion

What can one say about contemporary American religious cultures? Has American religion changed in the last 70 years? Can one discuss "American religion" as if it were an undifferentiated whole? And, given that the term itself has no stable meaning, can we even pick out some social formation we call "religion" that can be separately examined as a field apart from "culture," "politics," or other categories we might construe? The practices, institutions, and concepts that these words are supposed to represent are blurrily intermingled, for sure. Here I will do my best to draw attention to this ambiguity while striving for clarity in my description of the present. The period since the 1950s has been rife with legal and political battles over the place of religion in the public sphere. Polemics have often trumped—but also molded—the findings that surface in polling, surveys, qualitative studies, and religion journalism. Sociologists, pollsters, and journalists (because they usually define "religion" as institutional and as a divisible part of "culture") point to several trends.[32] The major ones include the numerical decline of so-called mainline Protestant denominations and the growth in theologically conservative ones (and more theologically open ones, such as Neopaganism), the increase in "switching" religious groups during one's lifespan, a rising cohort of Americans who belong to no religious groups (all disparately lumped together under the moniker "nones"), and the increasing visibility of those who combine religious idioms (think of a Methodist who believes in reincarnation).[33] Add to these a host of other changes, including the increased presence of Asian religions (enabled by a 1965 change in immigration laws), the expanded access to religious materials enabled by mass media technologies, the rise of evangelical seeker and megachurches along the beltways of New South and midwestern cities, the declining importance of denominational identity and theological particularities, the deepening connections between white evangelicals and the Republican Party, and the increase in those who tell pollsters that they believe in angels, demons, and ghosts. The list is long, and the theme—like that of a self-help book—is transformation (even if the relationships between religion and variables such as race, gender, class, and region have changed very little).[34]

The scholarly portrayals of these changes, trends, and visibilities are also myriad. Dwelling to seeking, melting pots becoming tossed salads, spiritual marketplaces, and pick and mix candy cabinets are just a few of the many phrases, terms, and metaphors used to describe American religion and its shifts since the 1950s. There are multiple ways—complementary and contradictory—in which one might describe contemporary American culture and its religions.[35] For my purposes here, I offer three characterizations: the consumerist, the haunted, and the therapeutic. These certainly aren't the only tropes for understanding something out there called "contemporary American culture," nor are they necessarily better descriptions than other classifications, depending upon one's focus and the questions being asked. But I do suggest that they provide very useful lenses through which to look at some prominent discourses that permeate contemporary social institutions and individual habits.

The first, the consumerist, suggests that contemporary Americans are immersed in what might be described as a "consuming convert's republic," to reference and revise the title from Lizabeth Cohen's work on the rise of consumer capitalism in the postwar United States, *A Consumer's Republic*.[36] The era from World War II to the present has witnessed a shift from a predominantly industrial to a consumption-fuelled form of capitalism. In other words, heavy industry, such as steel, constitutes a declining portion of the U.S. gross national product, with an increasing portion devoted to consumer and service items, such as clothing, mp3 players, and deodorant.. This has resulted in what the demographer Cheryl Russell refers to as a "personalized economy."[37] This can be described as a marketplace that increasingly produces multiple and minor variations of commodities in an effort to sell customers items that promote their own unique "individuality." And, if we believe some social scientists, individuality—or better, "identity"—is now something we need to work on. Pointing to shifts in unstable labor markets, increasing geographic mobility, and changing notions of community and intimacy, writers such as the social theorist Anthony Giddens argue that our identities in this "late modern" era are less ascribed by family, occupation, and place of origin and more a task we need to perform, a "project of the self" that "becomes translated into one of the possession of desired goods and the pursuit of artificially framed styles of life."[38] "Now," writes the sociologist of religion Robert Wuthnow, "because their roles are not predefined, individuals have to worry about who they are, who they want to be, and how they want other people to perceive them."[39] More and more, the sociological narrative goes, individuals from all social locations seek their identities and communities through increasingly segmented yet ubiquitous mass-media and niche-market consumer goods. And it's not just toothpaste. As noted by the religion scholars Jeremy Carrette and Richard King, "following the deregulation of markets by Margaret Thatcher and Ronald Reagan and the rise of neoliberalism as the global ideology of our age, cultural forms have themselves become commodities."[40] At a time when identities are less ascribed by family, history, occupation, and community, the notion that people may— indeed must—"choose" the lifestyle with which to identify themselves is propelled and compelled by consumer capitalism, mass-mediated culture divorced from historical contextualization, and the increasing authority and trust individuals give to their own subjective experience.

Given these assertions (and some statistical evidence to back them), it is not surprising that many social scientists now refer to religion as a product to be bought, used, and discarded when it isn't working (or when you become aware of a version that better accessorizes with your lifestyle). This "spiritual marketplace," as the sociologist of religion Wade Clark Roof dubs it, is filled with "consumers" who actively pick, mix, and combine the religious idioms that tickle their spiritual fancies—and do it in a way that "decultures" and "dehistoricizes" religious materials.[41] In other words, religious idioms such as reincarnation increasingly get taken out of their primary historical traditions and communities and mixed with other concepts and practices. Likewise, some scholars think of religious groups themselves as "marketers" who promote what the scholar Mara Einstein calls "brands of faith" with the hopes of gaining customers.[42] As argued by the sociologist of religion Andrew McKinnon, some social scientists and journalists use marketing terms to describe the religious field in such a way that they are no longer metaphors; rather, they become descriptions that naturalize the neoliberal conception of autonomous, freely willed, and fully cognizant individuals—profit-maximizing agents who make rational choices to get the religious products that best suit their needs.[43] At some extremes, these "rational choice" and "religious economy" theories of religion read like handbooks written by marketing firms, how-to guides containing predictive tools and suggestions for garnering more converts than your competitors.[44]

Whatever terms we use to describe it, however we decide to bemoan or praise it, the consumer capitalist economy reverberates in institutions, languages, practices, and the daily interactions of individuals in their work, leisure, and love lives. "Amid the hyperpluralism of divergent truth claims, metaphysical beliefs, moral values, and life priorities," writes the historian Brad Gregory, "ubiquitous practices of consumerism are more than anything else the cultural glue that holds Western society together." Even protests against the market, Gregory points out, "whether in books by astute intellectuals or songs by angry pop artists, are rendered innocuous precisely by being successfully marketed and sold. Capitalism liquefies all because it incorporates all."[45] Our identities are shaped by our consumer actions and our consuming desires. So why would we think that what we call "religion" would not be? I agree with Kathryn Lofton's assertion that "to study modern religion—to study the modern American economy—requires thinking of these categories as conjoined, and not distinct."[46] Recent examinations of Wal-Mart, Italian monastic communities, Cambridge metaphysicals, New Age Channelers, and the movement of guru Sathya Sai Baba all provide case studies of the intertwining and inextricability of religion and market.[47] Within the consuming convert's republic, it's not just that we have little choice but to shop and buy, but that the forceful sustain of consumer capitalism shapes our conversations, habits, relationships, and fantasies.

We are possessed by our possessions, but we seem susceptible to other types of possession as well. Ghosts, demons, and other spirits appear to be consuming some Americans' time, haunting their houses, and invading their bodies. A second characterization of the contemporary American imaginary, the haunted present, describes this vibrant and increasingly visible interest in the supernatural and paranormal, as seen in everything from surveys to television series and purchasable ghost-hunting kits. Polls suggest that between one-third and one-half of all Americans are either certain or think it probable that ghosts exist. An even larger number (68 percent), "completely" or "mostly" agree that angels and demons are active in the world.[48] In some ways, we all live in a ghost-hunting reality television show now.[49] And in an era of niche-media marketing, the choices for the specific program in which to reside are multiple. Since the middle of the first decade of this century, there have been more than two dozen ghost-related reality series on American cable television. Thirteen of these could be found—either with new episodes or repeats—on expanded cable during a single week in the summer of 2013. The two recurrent program styles entail amateur (and amateur-like) video camera footage of nighttime hunts and staged revenant reenactments interspersed with interviews of the haunted. Some shows, such as *Ghosthunters*, feature little discussion of what most viewers would think of as "religion," while in others, such as *Paranormal State* and *A Haunting*, it plays large roles.[50] Those interested in ghost tourism can watch *Scariest Places on Earth* on the Travel Channel. Viewers with more specific paranormal tastes might pick the college hauntings program *School Spirits*. *The Haunted Collector* features possessed objects ranging from false teeth to dolls, while Animal Planet's *The Haunted* specializes in the supernatural torments of pets and their owners. *Celebrity Ghost Stories*, *Haunted Highways*, and *Psychic Kids: Children of the Paranormal* illustrate just a few of the other viewing pleasures for those interested in spirits familiar and unfamiliar, good and evil.[51]

While these ghost-hunting reality shows vary, the dominant aesthetic is one of slow wane. In *Paranormal State*, *The Haunted*, *Dead Files*, and others, the settings are small rural towns in Pennsylvania, Indiana, North Carolina, Kentucky, and Alabama. The population is dwindling, the paint is peeling off the 1920s bungalow housing stock, and the leafless trees suggest a perpetual autumn. The victims are usually working-class individuals and families being harassed by forces beyond their everyday vision and reach. The decay and dilapidation ramp up when the cameras turn away from individuals' homes and toward larger structures and institutions. Ghost hunters traipse through abandoned and condemned factories, hospitals, prisons, and schools, their infra-red cameras and digital recorders ready to capture a fading image or faint sound of a livelier past.[52] The detail of every haunting is different. Sometimes the spiritual culprit is an abusive father who refuses to go to hell; other times they are the ghosts of slaves who are angered that their history of suffering has been ignored.[53] But while the specifics vary, the stories are also very similar in that they feature something "uncanny," something the psychoanalyst Sigmund Freud described as "nothing new or foreign, but something familiar and old—established in the mind that has been estranged only by the process or repression."[54] While the consuming convert's republic stresses autonomous consumers freed from past histories and entanglements, the haunted present ambivalently suggests that the spirits of history, family, community, and institutional structures cannot be discarded but continue to haunt the present. In the contemporary period, supernatural entities signal a "return of the repressed" in which, to quote the scholar Judith Richardson, "things usually forgotten, discarded, or repressed become foregrounded, whether as items of fear, regret, explanation, or desire."[55] In the case of the haunted present, the repressed that returns seems to be history itself, with all of its familial, social, and material entanglements.

A third characterization of the contemporary period—and one that intertwines with the consumerist and haunted themes—is the therapeutic. The social theorist Eva Illouz argues that a therapeutic discourse permeates modern Western institutions such as business corporations, the family unit, mass media, and the nation-state. Whereas earlier forms of psychology focused on diagnosing and containing what it viewed as illness, modern therapeutic discourse focuses on caring for, improving upon, and "optimizing" one's feelings, attitudes, and relationships. The therapeutic demonstrates the increasing importance of the personal—feelings, subjective experience—and the idea that solutions to problems (either personal or global) must come from inside, through our attitudes about things more than any particular social actions. "The self," Ilouz argues, "has become the prime site for the management of the contradictions of modernity, and psychology has offered techniques to manage those contradictions."[56] Therapeutic discourse asserts that everyone is vulnerable, needs improvement, and thus the modern self is viewed as the problem *and* solution for the ills of contemporary life.

Self-help literature and its inculcation of "appropriate" emotions and positive mental attitudes serves as one major tool in the quest for stable identities and well-being. But scholars have also noted the use of therapeutic language and praxis within religious groups and movements, ranging from New Age practitioners to conservative

Protestants, from mainline Protestant pastoral counselors to Oprah Winfrey. Self-realization *is* salvation in many strands of contemporary American religion, and even a theologically conservative evangelical such as Joel Osteen assures audiences that "you can live your best life now," while fellow evangelical Rick Warren suggests keeping a reflexive journal to ensure that you have a successful "purpose-driven life." This intense focus on the private and personal—what the sociologist Phillip Hammond dubbed the "Third Disestablishment" of American religion—registers in Americans' contemporary combinative practices as well as their decreased interest in dogmatic denominational details.[57] Within the therapeutic ethos it's all about you . . . or me . . . but not *us*. And how we feel about things on the inside trumps any pesky external realities. In a mass-mediated world filled with competing claims and partisan echo chambers, if we don't feel like something is "true" (whether the "it" be theological minutiae such as trinitarian theology or the belief in the necessity of baptism, or empirical matters such as the statistical certainty of global warming or the lack of physical evidence for the existence of ghosts), then chances are we can access material that will support and supplement our hunches.[58]

＊　＊　＊

The four chapters that make up the rest of *American Possessions* provide discussion and analysis of Third Wave spiritual warfare, a particular kind of evangelical imaginary that reflects and is shaped by the consumerist, haunted, and therapeutic discourses discussed above. The first three chapters mirror the topics found in spiritual warfare handbooks. Chapter one, "Delivering the World," focuses on Third Wave views of demonic activity in American popular culture, the nation-state and its politics, and non-evangelical religions. Chapter two, "Possessed Possessions, Defiled Land, and the Horrors of History," examines Third Wave concerns with demon-possessed consumer objects, places, and land. Chapter three, "The Gothic Therapeutic," discusses how Third Wave deliverance manuals, first, register modern therapeutic discourse with a dark twist, and, second, complicate (neo)liberal notions of individual agency by focusing on how the works explain the demonization of individuals through willful sins, family inheritances, and traumatic experiences. The fourth chapter, "Haunting Desires: Agency in an Era of Possessions," concludes the work by discussing how the Third Wave imaginary's demonology ambivalently mirrors neoliberalism with regard to its desocialization, dehistoricization, and dematerialization of the world.

CHAPTER ONE

DELIVERING THE WORLD

Our world continues to grow smaller and smaller.
Rebecca Greenwood, Let Our Children Go

The gospel is authoritative and dogmatic. It will not compromise with evil or moral, social, or religious error.
Ed Murphy, The Handbook for Spiritual Warfare

Refuse to tolerate or back down.
Alice Patterson, Bridging the Racial and Political Divide

A pure heart is required for this level of intercession.
Rebecca Greenwood, Authority to Tread

Third Wave author Cindy Jacobs introduces her book *Deliver Us From Evil* by recounting a visit to a chain bookstore. As Jacobs entered the Colorado Springs shop and began browsing, she felt the Holy Spirit compelling her to enter the store's New Age section. Strolling through the full aisles, Jacobs was shocked by the large number of tarot cards, books about magic, and other items. "My head swam," she writes, "at the thought of so much occult material in my nice, Christian-influenced city."[1] Jacobs' experience is a near-perfect example of the Third Wave's ambivalence toward globalization, multiculturalism, neoliberal capitalism, and the multiplicity of goods and cultural materials that these things make available. For Third Wave writers, the shrinking world that accompanies transnational trade and cultural contact offers both promise and peril. The structures that make worldwide missionizing possible also open the doors to ungodly invasions at home, as the borders—geographical, cultural, interpersonal, and supernatural—that separate self from others bleed and mix.

The Third Wave's primary focus is spiritual warfare, the purpose of which is to banish demons from human bodies, material objects, local places, and whole regions of the globe. The most basic Third Wave goal is to deliver the world from Satan's minions and thus make it more receptive to Christ during what founder Peter Wagner calls the new "Second Apostolic Age." This term refers to the Third Wave belief that the twenty-first century is an era in which new apostles and prophets are receiving direct and world-changing revelations from Christ. In order to hasten the coming of God's kingdom "here on earth as it is in heaven," "charismatically inclined" Third Wave practitioners learn spiritual warfare from handbooks, workshops, and hands-on participation in deliverance sessions. They fight evil spirits in God's name on three levels: the ground (delivering individuals from oppressive demons), the occult (battling demonic movements such as satanism, witchcraft, freemasonry, and various non-evangelical religions), and the strategic (fighting territorial spirits who control entire regions and cultures).[2] These efforts to deliver the world inevitably entail intense and intimate interaction with the enemy and his demons, who control much of the earth. Dangers abound in this war, and the battle lines can be drawn anywhere: from children's toys and human bodies to buildings and cities, from foreign countries to one's own home.

Wherever spiritual warfare is fought, one prominent—if rarely discussed—motif is that of purification. And, as the anthropologist Webb Keane notes, "purification requires an opponent." For Third Wave writers, that opponent is always Satan, yet his visage appears in other peoples' religions, cultures, and politics. Spiritual warfare handbooks promote pure hearts, clean minds, dogmatic practices, and intolerant attitudes while simultaneously warning readers that devilish syncretisms and occult conspiracies want to foul the sacred. Spiritual warfare enthusiastically marks boundaries, divides pure from impure, distinguishes orthodox from heretical, and separates godly from satanic. But these purifying practices often just make explicit the hybrid, combined, and blended status of Third Wave theology and practice. The historian of science Bruno Latour writes that, "the more we forbid ourselves to conceive of hybrids, the more possible their interbreeding becomes."[3] Registering what the American religious studies scholar Jason Bivins aptly dubs the "erotics of fear" and the "demonology within," the Third Wave imaginary is attracted to that which repulses it; it mimics the demonic while hoping to defeat it. In other words, in fighting the amorphous occult and its evil entities, Third Wave rituals and conceptions mirror that of its enemy. "It is precisely amid the strongest efforts to clarify religious orthodoxy and identity," Bivins writes, "when the religious stakes seem highest. . . . Boundaries are blurred in the very effort to clarify them."[4]

In this chapter, I map, in Third Wave writings, the process that Bivins describes. I do this by discussing the boundaries that spiritual warfare handbook writers mark between the satanic and the godly. The Third Wave imaginary finds the demonic in other peoples' religions, including other forms of Christianity and especially Roman Catholicism. Indigenous cultures encountered in the mission field and American popular cultures confronted in one's own home (and especially in children's possessions and bedrooms) also house evil spirits.[5] Political parties harbor the demonic. Third Wave authors warn of syncretistic occult conspiracies that include satanists, Masons, Wiccans, New Agers, college students, and hospital employees. In a time of increased globalization, cultural tolerance, and the consumer items that come with these things, spiritual warfare manuals assert that no Christian is safe anywhere. But in laying out the practical demonologies and ritual actions to defend the world from Satan's minions, I argue that Third Wave handbooks mirror the hybrid and world-tainted grimoires (books of magical spells and invocations to hail spirits), activities, and popular-culture materials that their authors and readers so fiercely seek to exorcise. Similarly, evangelicals who critique the Third Wave don't succeed in marking boundaries between orthodoxy and heresy in spiritual warfare, but rather expose the connections and shared assumptions between theological relatives. In the end, the Third Wave (and any other) campaign for purity reveals that such a state doesn't exist. Instead, the very crusade for purity exposes its own hybrid, melded constitution.

OTHER PEOPLES' RELIGIONS

In *The Third Wave of the Holy Spirit*, Peter Wagner tells readers about the miracle of the flaming dung. In the tale, a "witch doctor" in Mandala, India, received a flyer from a missionary with a picture of Jesus on it. He placed the flyer on his shelf, next to representations of other gods. After some time, Wagner relates, the witch doctor "was beginning to think that Jesus was the one true God, but he needed a test." He decided to place a small amount of dried cow feces in front of each picture, thinking that the most powerful god would ignite the manure. While dried cow dung is used for domestic fires, it also serves as fuel for some Indian ritual offerings. "Almost immediately," Wagner writes, "the dung in front of Jesus' picture burst into flames." The miracle of the flaming dung was so striking that the "witch doctor" became "a fervent evangelist for Jesus Christ."[6]

In the Third Wave imaginary, Jesus is the one true God, and physical demonstrations of this abound in mission fields and at home: dung miraculously ignites in India, rotten teeth are healed in South America, and the "deaf and dumb" are cured in the United States. In spiritual warfare manuals, other peoples' religions aren't just false and weak, they are dangerous and demonic. The Guatemalan pastor and spiritual warfare author Harold Caballeros writes that Satan "originated different religions" in order to "extract" power from humans, while the intercessor Rebecca Greenwood tells readers that "idolatrous worship is the main reason behind the shedding of innocent blood, adultery, moving God's earth boundaries, changing the laws of God, not asking God for wisdom and killing righteous people."[7] Of course, the fact that this form of evangelicalism—or any number of other religions for that matter—demonizes other peoples' religions isn't the least bit surprising. In the case of the Third Wave, one might add that the demonization is both especially virulent and literal. Other peoples' religions were birthed by the devil and supervised by his management team of evil spirits.

Scholars of American religion have written much in recent years on the subject of religious diversity and pluralism. While the social formations, practices, and concepts that may be dubbed "religious" have always been diverse in North America, the contemporary era of globalization and transnationalism makes the subject seem more pertinent than ever. Some scholars have chosen to celebrate American religious diversity, others delineate pluralism's history, and a few consider the politics and meanings of such terms and concepts.[8] The authors of spiritual warfare handbooks are aware of the diverse American religious landscape, and they are clear in their intense dislike of it. The Third Wave evangelical counselor Ed Murphy, for example, bemoans cultural pluralism as an American problem, asserting that "often cultural pluralism in the form of political correctness seeks to silence any clear witness to the Christ event." Given this, it is not surprising that in addition to telling tales of Thai Buddhist temple demons and Bangladeshi storm spirits, Third Wave intercessors busy themselves in the United States by praying against the building of Muslim temples, citing the Talmud as an example of superstition, and warning readers to pray against Hindu demons because they are now "widespread in our nation."[9]

But of course it isn't just non-Christian religions that are demonized. Spiritual warfare manuals, like the larger genre of evangelical anti-cult literature, warn readers about the dangers of liberal Protestants (because, writers say, they deny the realities of the supernatural world) and unnamed "Christian cults" (because, it is claimed, they aren't really Christian at all). But more than any other world religion, such as Islam or Hinduism, or any other form of Christianity, Third Wave writers focus their demon-banishing missiles at Roman Catholicism. As works by the historians John Higham, Jenny Franchot, John Corrigan, Lynn Neal, and others attest, North American Protestants inherited a particularly virulent strain of anti-Catholicism from their European forebears.[10] Anti-Catholic rhetoric and activities are a constant in American history. They were present in Puritan law, antebellum literature such as *The Awful Disclosures of Maria Monk*, early-twentieth-century Ku Klux Klan materials, and even during the 2004 American presidential election, when a small North Carolina Pentecostal church handed out flyers suggesting that the Catholic candidate John Kerry would "ban" Bibles. While scholars such as Michael Lienesch, William Martin, and Seth Dowland have written about the late-twentieth-century Christian Right's alliance with Roman Catholics in anti-abortion politics, Third Wave evangelicals remain explicitly anti-Catholic.[11]

Spiritual warfare manuals pay particular heed to Roman Catholics' demon-haunted material culture. Readers are warned to avoid items such as rosary beads and iconography, where demons are especially likely to lurk. Eddie Smith, for example, tells a story of how the Holy Spirit spoke to him while he was missionizing in Latvia. The crucifix, it said, was hindering the spiritual growth of the people there. When Smith asked why, he wrote that "I felt the Holy Spirit say, 'the crucifix is a "photograph" of Satan's finest hour.'" "Whether carved in wood, chiseled in stone, painted in oils or molded in bronze," the Holy Spirit told Smith, "the crucifix presents to the world a dead, helpless God, which provokes many to pity and few to faith." Smith concludes his story by telling readers that, the following night, he explained the revelation to the congregation at the church where he was preaching. The parishioners responded by removing the crucifixes they were wearing. "All heavens broke loose," he recounts, "people were born again and delivered."[12]

Smith's concern with portraying Christ as "weak, emaciated, sickly, or dead," evokes long-running debates in American religious history over the portrayal of Jesus. As noted by the religion and visual culture scholar David Morgan, early-twentieth-century proponents of "muscular Christianity" expressed concern that many graphic representations of Jesus were not masculine enough. For example, Bruce Barton, an advertising executive, Republican politician, and Christian book author, railed against portrayals of Jesus as a "physical weakling" and touted his image as a burly and hairy outdoorsman.[13] Third Wave evangelicals, in criticizing the crucifix, claim that to portray Jesus as injured and in pain is to promote the devil's temporary triumph. In writing that "the Cross was not a tragedy, it was a victory," Smith suggests that the Catholic crucifix—rather than portraying an ultimate sacrifice—shows a point of weakness that was "Satan's finest hour."

And it's not just Catholic objects that are likely to be haunted. Third Wave writers assert that Roman Catholic family and folk practices are inviting to demons. Intercessor and Apostle Cindy Jacobs suggests, for example, that "you can be cursed by being named after a saint" and warns that "sometimes the worship of a particular saint in a family line is so strong that a person needs to make a clean break and change his or her name."[14] Catholic folk practices such as the Cult of San La Muerte, "Saint Death," which is found primarily in Latin American countries and communities, also receive attention in spiritual warfare handbooks. In one story, Peter Wagner suggests that San La Muerte was one of several territorial spirits who had control over the Argentinian city of Resistencia. Wagner took a spiritual warfare team to battle the demons with prayer and revival services. His story concludes gruesomely—and in Wagner's telling victoriously—when God apparently kills a leading San La Muerte devotee. Two weeks after the warfare had commenced, Wagner reports, the "high priestess" of San La Muerte in Resistencia died in a fire in which the flames selectively "consumed only the mattress, the woman, and her statue of San La Muerte!"[15] Exulting in a woman's death may seem perverse, but for Wagner it is not a tragedy but a triumph, victory over the enemy, who is a casualty of spiritual warfare.

The Catholic (Roman and orthodox) subject that receives the most attention from these writers is the Virgin Mary. In Third Wave spiritual warfare manuals, the Mary of Catholic iconography and devotion is not actually the mother of Jesus, but is instead identified as the evil "Queen of Heaven," one of the most powerful "demonic principalities" on earth.[16] "Queen of Heaven" is indeed a Roman Catholic term for Mary, but it was also used in antiquity for goddesses such as Isis and Astarte, and Third Wave writers focus on this connection. Rebecca Greenwood tells readers that Satan "has succeeded in infiltrating the Roman Catholic Church with this deception" and that the

Queen of Heaven is responsible for innumerable horrors, including the murder of Jews during the Crusades, the violence of the Spanish Inquisition, and the mass genocide of the Holocaust. Spiritual warfare handbooks invariably include stories of successful "battles" against demons, and some of these focus on skirmishes against the Queen of Heaven and her demonic hordes. In such tales, intercessors invade "enemy territories" such as Santa Maria Maggiore Church in Rome or, in the Ukraine, an underground tomb of Russian Orthodox saints devoted to Mary.[17] Their warfare prayers and songs at these sites lead to the lifting of "feelings of heaviness" in the air, as well as occasional conversions of Catholic worshipers and tourists. Often, such as in the case of the Resistencia fire, Third Wave writers point to dramatic and sometimes violent physical events that signal God's presence and His unhappiness with Catholic belief, worship, and ritual. In one such story, Peter Wagner tells how a local Catholic priest in an Argentinian city protested the crusade Wagner's group had initiated by "invading the area with a religious procession." "When they arrived," Wagner writes, "the four strong men carrying the statue of the priest's favorite virgin all fell to the ground under the power of the Spirit and the statue shattered into a thousand pieces."[18] Wagner concludes by asserting that two of the men were hospitalized by the fall, while the other two were delivered and saved at the crusade.

OTHER PEOPLES' CULTURES AND AMERICAN POPULAR CULTURE

But it isn't just other peoples' religions that pose problems. Other peoples' cultures can also play host to the demonic and engulf members of the society. "Generally speaking from a biblical perspective," writes Ed Murphy in *The Handbook for Spiritual Warfare*, "there exist three different broad types of cultural components: those compatible with Christian faith, those incompatible, and those neutral."[19] F. Douglas Pennoyer, coeditor with Peter Wagner of the influential 1990 manual *Wrestling with Dark Angels*, suggests that "cultural systems are not inherently evil, but the combined activity of demonized individuals, leading others in traditionally demonic focused activities, creates collective captivity." This "collective captivity" ties people to the demonic through everyday and presumedly innocent cultural practices, ideas, and rites. In spiritual warfare handbooks, indigenous peoples are often the targets of such claims. Pennoyer, for example, offers a case study of the Tawbuid of the Philippines. In societies like theirs, Pennoyer asserts, "all social, political, economic, religious and even artistic subsystems of culture are actively manipulated and controlled by demons acting through individuals . . . all transitions in the life cycle—for example birth, puberty, marriage, and death—are surrounded with evil spirit rituals."[20] For Murphy, Pennoyer, and other practitioners of spiritual warfare, some aspects of peoples' cultures are fine, but others must be rejected and replaced by "components compatible with the gospel."[21] When it comes to indigenous cultures, however, what is salvageable and what is demonic is not always clear, as will be seen later.

For Third Wave evangelicals, American popular culture poses greater risks than foreign cultures because of its proximity and ability to attract one's own children. American religion scholars have pointed out that members of conservative forms of Protestantism have often been the most vocal critics of popular culture, rhetorically espousing a wariness toward the world and often prohibiting activities such as dancing, watching movies, and listening to certain forms of music. At the same time, Pentecostals, charismatics, and other evangelicals have frequently embraced new media technologies and popular-culture styles for missionizing purposes.[22] "Rather than serving as an oppositional other from which to push off and consolidate a separate identity," writes the sociologist Lynne Gerber, "American culture is also the locus of evangelical identification and appropriation."[23] Overall, American evangelicals have exhibited ambivalence toward American popular culture, seeking to fully participate—whether through such things as Christian rock, Christian self-help literature, or Christian children's television programming—while also expressing concern that much popular culture is a tool of Satan that welcomes the demonic.

As will be discussed in chapter two, Third Wave writers assert that physical objects such as DVDs, CDs, jewelry, and statues can house demons. But certain popular-culture styles also harbor the satanic. Horror films, "occult" fiction such as Harry Potter books and movies, and "occult" television shows such as *The Smurfs* and *Bewitched* all garner attention. Rebecca Greenwood writes of music,

> Many styles of music are purely satanic in nature and are meant to per- petuate the lies of Satan. I have heard the argument that the lyrics of songs and even satanic music cannot harm or influence those who listen to them. This is not true. Secular news media have reported how many teenagers, after attending rock concerts led by Satanists, returned home to commit suicide.[24]

Given both scholarship and popular press depictions from the post– World War II period to the present, it is not surprising to find out that musical styles such as hard rock, metal, and punk most frequently get singled out in Third Wave manuals as being dangerous to one's spiritual state.[25] From evangelical suggestions that playing satanic record albums backward would reveal the voices of demons, to the Parents' Music Resource Center crusade against the dangers of heavy metal, music with distorted guitars and medium-to-fast tempos has always—especially when it has appealed to youth—been the primary focus.[26] In *Deliver Us From Evil*, Cindy Jacobs warns readers that "heavy-metal music is a huge doorway into the occult," and asks par- ents whether their children are listening to "Black Sabbath, AC/DC, Marilyn Manson, KISS, or some other heavy-metal group?" Never mind that bands such as AC/DC and KISS are seldom thought of as "heavy metal" by music fans. And never mind that Third Wave writ- ers such as Jacobs rarely if ever mention actual self-described Satanist bands such as Akercocke, or even explicitly anti-Christian ones such as some found in the Norwegian black metal scene. These are obscure bands who sell few records and remain unknown to spiritual warfare authors. Instead, writers focus on more mainstream groups and figures that are widely known, such as Marilyn Manson.

For example, in *Authority to Tread: An Intercessor's Guide to Strategic Level Spiritual Warfare*, Rebecca Greenwood describes how her spiritual warfare group shut down a Marilyn Manson concert in Houston through the power of prayer. Manson, the Alice Cooper–like performer who was falsely tied to the 1999 Columbine High School massacre by some popular media outlets, sold millions of records and garnered a good deal of negative attention from some evangelical and conservative commentators in the 1990s and early 2000s. Greenwood, after suggesting that Manson's music glorifies Satan and has caused a rash of teen suicides, related how God led her warfare group, stationed outside the concert hall, to pray that the sound system would not work. Their prayer was answered when "one of the fans spilled his beer on the soundboard," which short-circuited the entire sound system and forced the concert to be abruptly stopped.[27]

For Third Wave writers, the styles, clothing, and bodily aesthetics that accompany rock and metal music also come under scrutiny. Rebecca Greenwood informs readers that tattoos and piercings are related to demonic oppression, while Cindy Jacobs suggests that two of the thirty-six warning signs that your child is into the occult includes a "preoccupation with black clothing" and wearing silver jewelry instead of gold. And according to Greenwood, "Emo," the vaguely bounded genre associated with bands such as Hawthorne Heights and My Chemical Romance, is "doing Satan's work" and leads teens who are into the music to cut themselves. In *Let Our Children Go: Steps to Free your Child from Evil Influences and Demonic Harassment*, she tells parents that it is crucial that they pray with their children for repentance from cutting, because, "if there has been cutting and bloodshed, this gives more power to the demonic."[28]

OTHER PEOPLES' POLITICS

While some Third Wave leaders such as Peter Wagner have spoken guardedly about American politics in nonreligious media outlets, others have been much more explicit in pointing out the demonic nature of the federal government.[29] Conservative politicians and media notables such as Sarah Palin, Pat Robertson, David Barton, Ted Haggard, and Rick Perry either have associations with or share language and understandings of the world that reflects the influence of Third Wave spiritual warfare and/or its most explicitly political submovement, the New Apostolic Reformation, which appears to be a more extreme version of the Christian Right. Some Third Wave figures such as Alice Patterson and Cindy Jacobs argue that diversity and tolerance are dangerous and provide a theological demonization of the Democratic Party and an apologetics for the Republican Party.

As the United States becomes visibly more diverse in terms of race and religion, and more tolerant and accepting of civil rights for lesbian, gay, bisexual, and transgender (LGBT) persons, some Third Wave writers have suggested that such diversity and toleration are demonic. The intercessor and New Apostolic Reformation prophet Cindy Jacobs, like many within the movement, believes that the United States was founded as a Christian country and asserts that "democracy without the basic doctrines of the Bible eventually deteriorates into a society led by a military dictatorship or other types of non-democratic governments." New Apostolic Reformation/spiritual warfare proponent Alice Patterson, also like many others in the Christian Right, ignores (or is ignorant of) American history, the First Amendment's Establishment Clause, Madison and Jefferson's writings, and constitutional law when she writes that "some of us may have been brought into the doctrine of the separation of church and state, although the concept is foreign to our constitution." In such a worldview, to tolerate (let alone embrace) lifestyles, religions, and government policies that contradict Third Wave conceptions of Christianity is to lay out a welcome mat for Satan and his demon soldiers. Jacobs warns parents not to be "intimidated by the modern-day culture of tolerance," telling them instead that "being intolerant of evil is a good thing, not a bad thing." "The opposite of tolerance is confrontation," writes Alice Patterson, "refuse to tolerate or back down. Confront. Expose. Uncover. Make known."[30]

Patterson, the founder of the San Antonio–based Justice at the Gate organization, gained some notoriety in left-wing media for her involvement with Texas governor Rick Perry's 2011 prayer rally.[31] Perry, who at the time was seeking the Republican presidential nomination, invited a number of New Apostolic Reformation/spiritual warfare figures to speak at the rally. Patterson's Justice at the Gate is an organization dedicated to racial reconciliation with the goal of bringing more African Americans into the Republican Party. Before forming this organization focused on "building strategic partnerships to mobilize Christians to pray effectively and to vote righteously," she was field director for the Texas Christian Coalition and the Texas coordinator for the U.S. Strategic Prayer Network.[32] While all of these organizations place her soundly within the political sphere of the New Christian Right, what garnered her press for being part of Perry's prayer rally was her 2010 work of political theology, *Bridging the Racial and Political Divide: How Godly Politics Can Transform a Nation*. It was in this work that Patterson provided an explicit spiritual warfare demonization of American politics.

In the book, Patterson relates that the impetus for her work came from listening to the well-known Third Wave figure Chuck Pierce speak at the 2004 U.S. Strategic Prayer Network Convention. Hearing Pierce talk about "Saul Structures," Patterson concluded that Pierce's description of demonized institutions perfectly described the Democratic Party. "This was the first time," she writes, "that I ever considered that an evil structure could be connected to and empowered by a political party." Patterson then prayed to God to reveal to her the demonic structure controlling the Democrats and found that it was "Jezebel," a rebellious female demon. Under Jezebel, Patterson elaborates, are two lesser demons: "Asherah," a "spirit who emasculates men and defeminizes women"; and "Baal," who encourages the worship of false gods. "Stay with me," Patterson urges, as she connects the demonic dots of Democratic politics, "as we see how the same three things: kissing the Baal for economic gain, the shedding of innocent blood and sexual immorality comprise the Jezebel structure hiding behind the Democratic Party today." For Patterson, the Democratic Party's support of slavery in the 1800s, its affirmation of the *Roe v. Wade* Supreme Court ruling, and its partial support for LGBT civil rights (or, in Patterson's description, its promotion of "sexual perversion") can thus be directly linked to the influence of the powerful demon Jezebel.

"Through her structure of demonic entities," Patterson writes, "Jezebel has succeeded in supplanting worship and faith in God with confusion and dependency on government resulting in generational poverty in those loyal to her."[33]

But it isn't just the Democrats who have demon troubles. For Patterson, Republicans are equally infested with something she calls the "Ahab structure," a demonic agent (named after a biblical king who was married to Jezebel) that causes Republicans to be too tolerant. In other words, Patterson suggests that the Republican Party is haunted by demons in a manner that makes it too compromising, accepting, and democratically deliberative. Patterson asserts that the "Republican Platform excels in virtue," but "Ahab surrenders and yields to intimidation," leading Republicans to "acquiesce, compromise, and give their authority away under the constant pounding by Democrats and the fear of what people will think and the media will write." Republican lawmakers, Patterson asserts, are driven by the demonic structure influencing their party to fear being labeled "intolerant, homophobic, racist, and uncaring," so they often hesitate to support the policies that Patterson sees as morally correct. Because the demonic Ahab structure compels toleration and compromise, the Republicans "don't have a killer instinct," something desperately needed, because "we must not be merciful to Jezebel or the governmental structure she's empowering."[34]

Patterson's arguments may look to outsiders like those of a partisan crackpot. But her political demonology looks reasonable and accurate to many within the Third Wave. While Peter Wagner was hesitant to affirm Patterson's views during a 2011 National Public Radio interview, he did provide a laudatory blurb on the back of her 2010 book. And more than one journalist suggested that Rick Perry's decision to include Patterson at his prayer rally was in part a strategic move to win voters who were connected with Christian Right organizations. The evocation of Ahab and Jezebel, the explicit promotion of intolerance, and the attack on political compromise and discussion, suggest harmony between the Third Wave's New Apostolic Reformation and far right politics—a connection just as strong as that between the broader

Republican Party and more mainstream evangelicals.[35] Spiritual warfare is, among many other things, a language of martial conflict. That the enemy should be found in American politics, popular culture, and other peoples' religions and cultures is not surprising. The simplified either/or choices are good versus evil, Satan versus God, heaven versus hell. Living in the final days of life as we know it, as the Third Wave's apocalyptic theology suggests, spiritual warfare manual writers warn that there is ultimately a satanic conspiracy to rule the world, one that is most easily seen in the globalizing movements and activities that Third Wave authors label "New Age."

THE NEW AGE/OCCULT/SATANIST CONSPIRACY

Third Wave writers see the New Age movement as extremely dangerous. "Those in the New Age are taught that they can call upon the power of demonic forces in any religion in the world," writes Cindy Jacobs. "[T]hey are swiftly infiltrating schools in many nations in order to take over the minds of our children and set up their ideologies in local and national governments."[36] "It would be safe to assert that the greatest threat to Christianity in the world today is the New Age Movement," Ed Murphy concurs, "not Satanism, not the revival of traditional religions like Islam, not even secular humanism."[37] In spiritual warfare handbooks, the New Age is viewed as one of Satan's most effective global conspiracies, one that permeates popular culture, politics, and many other social institutions. The rhetoric of conspiracy found in Third Wave manuals sounds familiar to students of American history. Whether the culprit was asserted to be Freemasons, Mormons, Catholics, Communists, or Satanists, the accusations and narratives—as pointed out long ago by David Brion Davis and by many others since—have been remarkably similar.[38] The uniqueness of the conspiracies asserted by spiritual warfare writers involves two elements: first, the fact that all of the aforementioned groups are seen as being in cahoots, and, second, the groups are all assumed to be demon-infested and -controlled.

While the New Age is believed to be particularly dangerous, spiritual warfare manuals often lump the movement with "the occult" and "satanism" in an unholy trinity that colludes, combines, and envelops a wide variety of social formations. The occult—those movements, powers, and teachings hidden from everyday view—is, for Third Wave writers, a broad concept that encompasses everything from children's martial arts classes and yoga to Wiccans and Freemasons.[39] Rebecca Greenwood, for example, warns that "any participation in occult activity is a red carpet invitation for demons," and provides a two-page list of things that fall under the heading. She warns readers that Freemasonry "teaches that men become gods" and that all members are problematically "free to worship the deity of their choice and are told that the god they worship is the true way to eternal life." God's dislike of such pluralism is apparent, as Greenwood asserts that spirits of "death" and "infirmity" are common among Freemasons, and thus it is "not unusual for sudden, premature and unexpected deaths of active members to occur."[40]

Greenwood also focuses attention on Wicca, one of the fastest-growing religious movements in the United States today.[41] She suggests that a "fierce battle" is being waged on college and high school campuses as witchcraft groups missionize and recruit young members. Acknowledging that many Wiccans explicitly deny that they are satanists, Greenwood insists nonetheless that their "beliefs and practices are promoting the lies of Satan" and that they have unwittingly "become pawns of the enemy."[42] In a story related during a Michigan spiritual warfare conference, Peter Wagner described how one witch died, apparently through God's divine intervention, when she was persistent in protesting a local school board's use of Christian prayer in their meetings. In this tale, told to me by a college student who had attended the conference, the witch's attempt to stop the violation of the Establishment Clause of the First Amendment to the Constitution resulted in God's wrath. Whether the enemy is New Agers, Freemasons, or Wiccans, such stories suggest that promotion of pluralism, diversity, and combinative religious/supernaturalist practices are demonic and that toleration of such things gives succor to Satan. Indeed, the New Age movement and all things occult ultimately get placed in the Third Wave spiritual warfare taxonomy—despite conflating and at times confounding use of such terms—under the rubric "satanism." Ed Murphy writes,

> Satanism in the broadest sense of the word is contact with, worship of, homage to, and even use of spirit beings other than the one true God. This covers all of paganism, positive and negative witchcraft, occultism, and even non-Christian religions. While it is true that Judaism and Islam are theistic systems closely related to Christianity, they reject outright Jesus as Christ, Son of God, and Lord."[43]

Anything, then, that strays outside the Third Wave conception of Christianity (including other forms of Christianity such as Catholicism and liberal Protestantism) is satanic. At the same time, however, spiritual warfare manuals suggest that there are also self-identified Satanists at work in the world whose diabolical activities are not cloaked in the language and styles of combinative religions or fraternal organizations. By now much has been written about the satanism scares of the 1980s and early 1990s.[44] From television spectacles hosted by Geraldo Rivera and Sally Jesse Raphael to small-town rumor-driven panics in upstate New York and northern Ohio, stories circulated that there was an underground satanic network of individuals and groups who engaged in grave-robbing, child abduction, and human sacrifice. While sociological, criminological, and journalistic studies began debunking these rumors in the early 1990s, Third Wave authors—whose movement and manuals began to appear and multiply during the same period as the satanism scares—continue to report the tales as facts, even adding details. For example, in her 2001 work *Deliver Us From Evil*, Cindy Jacobs explicitly tells readers that scholars and FBI agents such as Kenneth Lanning who deny the existence of satanic conspiracies are wrong, that satanic ritual abuse and murders are real, and that she personally knows of "specific incidents in which little children have been abducted during preschool and used in occult rituals." Jacobs even suggests, in a flourish added to the genre of satanic legend, that satanists work at hospitals so that they can launch attacks on un-suspecting and ill Christians. She relates one story in which God tells a spiritual warfare intercessor to go to the hospital because a certain Christian was under "satanic attack." "When the intercessor arrived," Jacobs continues, "his friend was unattended and bleeding to death . . . it was later learned that the patient had seen a hospital attendant wear-ing an occult ring that bore a goat's head . . . they felt there was a connection." Jacobs tells readers that they should be on the alert when loved ones are in the hospital, because "there are occultists who work in medical facilities and, on occasion, they will use their position to advance the demonic cause."[45]

Such stories closely resemble contemporary urban legends. As noted by the folklorists Gary Alan Fine and Patricia Turner, tales about chain restaurants such as the "Kentucky Fried Rat" and the occasional and unfounded rumors that the Ku Klux Klan own Church's Fried Chicken, or about U.S. government involvement in spreading AIDS in poor black communities, stems in part from a distrust of distant and impersonal modern institutions and mass-produced consumer goods made in far-flung places.[46] Such anxieties are only enhanced in the Third Wave worldview, since conflict and satanic conspiracy are the-ological givens. "If we study the Bible, we will see that we live in a constant situation of spiritual warfare," writes Harold Caballeros in *Victorious Warfare*. "Spiritual warfare really constitutes the normal way of life for believers that have been redeemed by Christ from the slavery of the devil."[47]

THE IMPURITIES OF PURIFICATION

Third Wave spiritual warfare manuals "do" many kinds of work. One of their most important labors is to mark the boundaries between the godly and the satanic, between the demon-haunted and the righteous. "Syncretism"—the Christian missionary term for the melding of differ-ent religious systems together—is often decried as demonic. Religious/occult hybrids such as the New Age and Freemasonry are repeatedly mentioned as prime examples of satanic institutions. And, yet, spiritual warfare manuals and activities are themselves complex combinations of charismatic/Pentecostal Protestantism, popular and folk conceptions of the supernatural, and occult grimoires. Demons, of course, have long been part of Christianity, and Pentecostals have been busy banishing demons from human bodies since the movement was born in the first decade of the twentieth century.[48] But the details about demons in recent Third Wave handbooks owe as much to contemporary reality television shows as they do to the Bible.

Hauntings, as will be seen later, fill spiritual warfare manuals. The storylines resemble those found in programs such as *Paranormal State*, *The Haunted*, *Psychic Kids*, *My Ghost Story*, and most of the other dozens of syndicated ghost reality television shows.[49] The only difference is that, in Third Wave tales, what seem like ghosts are actually always demons. The close parallels suggest that the influence is mutual, with explicitly religious elements and pop/folk supernatural motifs blending together to create common tropes.[50] Alice Patterson, for example, relates a typical tale of haunting. After moving into a new house in 1979, Patterson began waking up in the middle of the night. When she entered her house's front bathroom, she was overcome by fear. Some neighbor friends eventually informed her that the previous owner had committed suicide in that bathroom. In response, Patterson writes,

> John and I prayed through the house. We applied the blood of Jesus all over it, especially in the bathroom. We commanded every evil spirit—especially suicide, death, and fear—to get out in the name of Jesus. . . . That's a pretty minor occurrence, but it validates the concept that demonic entities can inhabit a specific location.[51]

In its broad outlines, this sounds like any other ghost story. The exceptions, of course, have to do with the praying the blood of Jesus (a Pentecostal practice dating to the early twentieth century and discussed later in the book) and the nature of the entity in the bathroom. In terms of the latter, the main difference between Patterson's account and one you might see on ghost-hunting reality television is that, for

Third Wave evangelicals, there are no such things as ghosts. Theologically, what is haunting the house is not the ghost of its former owner but a demon.

At the same time, a significant number of ghost reality programs actually do include stories about demons, curses, and the occult. On *Paranormal State*, Ryan Buell and his ecumenical paranormal team of Catholics, Wiccans, and psychics have numerous episodes in which they investigate demonic spirits. And demons appear regularly on shows such as *A Haunting*, *The Haunted*, *Paranormal Witness*, *Ghost Adventures*, and *Psychic Kids: Children of the Paranormal*. Third-Waver Rebecca Greenwood mirrors a theme in these shows when she describes how a demon harassed her daughter regularly at 3:00 a.m.. Paranormal investigators on both television and the internet refer to this as the "haunting hour" or "devil's hour," when evil spirits are strongest. The belief stems from a legend that it was at 3:00 in the morning that Jesus died on the cross.[52] This hour, the moment furthest from that act of salvation, is thus prime time for evil. And so we see the merging of Christianity and folk beliefs.

Spiritual warfare handbooks and ghost reality television share a number of other motifs, particularly surrounding children. Both ghost hunters and Third Wave intercessors agree that children in general are especially adept at sensing spirits. It is a theme seen not just in child-focused programs such as *Psychic Kids*, which focuses on "training" children to accept and control their abilities to see and communicate with spirits, but also on *Paranormal Witness*, *The Haunted*, *Paranormal State*, and other shows. Greenwood argues, "the children who begin seeing or hearing in the spirit realm and dreaming dreams at young ages are those the Lord has gifted in prophecy, intercession, and discernment."[53] Ghost-hunting reality shows have less to say about prophecy, but do suggest that discernment of spirits may be more common among kids. Similarly, both warn readers/viewers that your child's imaginary friends could be evil spirits. Cindy Jacobs, for example, cautions readers that imaginary friends might be "a spirit guide trying to attach itself to your child—not just the child being cute." Greenwood even suggests that children must repent for having an imaginary playmate, since it could be a demon. Other shared tropes include the reality of demon-inspired human shapeshifting, astral projection, and the dangers of disturbing occult altars and sites without proper spiritual defenses.[54] Such themes and plots float freely between Third Wave spiritual warfare, paranormal television, and folk/popular legends, influencing and blending into each other so much as to become variations on the same story.

In addition to shared supernatural themes, Third Wave spiritual warfare manuals resemble—and even cite—the occult grimoires they attack as demonic. Most handbook authors acknowledge this and include an introductory statement in which they defend their books by saying that there are "flaky" (a common term in numerous manuals) spiritual warfare tomes out there, but that the one you are holding is certainly not one of them. Spiritual mapping specialist George Otis Jr. warns readers that the "boundaries between faith and superstition is exceedingly narrow and often crossed," while Eddie and Alice Smith respond to critics who think their manual on "spiritual housecleaning" sounds like superstition by asserting that "to us, superstition is placing faith in any person, place or thing other than the almighty God and His infallible Word."[55] Third Wave writers only vaguely mark the boundaries of flaky and serious, but always firmly place themselves on the sober side.

Scholars such as Bill Ellis, Jason Bivins, and David Frankfurter have pointed out that the activities and materials of witch hunters, demonologists, and cult specialists frequently mirror those of the evil others they seek to out and banish.[56] Some spiritual warfare manuals go further, citing "satanic" works to support arguments. In *Informed Intercession*, Otis positively references works from the Neopagan/New Age press Llewellyn to assert the reality of "ley lines" and "earthlights."[57] In several ways, spiritual warfare manuals themselves can be accurately described as "grimoires," books of magical spells and invocations to hail spirits. Third Wave handbooks contain incantations (prayers) that seek to call up, bind, and ultimately banish evil spirits. And, like American hoodoo and conjure traditions, these works are (obviously) heavily saturated with Christian language and biblical references.

Third Wave writers answer such criticisms by pointing out that the intention of spiritual warfare, and more crucially the supernatural power on which it draws, make all the difference. What distinguishes these actions from mere superstition is that they are taken in Jesus' name and have God's force behind them. Past debates in American religious history touched on the appropriateness of particular rituals and practices. While one might immediately cite twentieth-century evangelical Protestant arguments over whether Pentecostal glossolalia (speaking in tongues) signaled possession by the Holy Spirit or by a demon, a better comparison would be the New England Puritans.[58] The Puritans of the Massachusetts Bay Colony lived in a world alive with supernatural powers.[59] They consulted astrologers to determine their fates, utilized talismans and charms to heal their pains, and waved their Bibles over crops while speaking sacred prayers to stimulate growth. While the clergy frowned upon the use of "judicial" astrology to foretell human fates and talismans to heal human bodies, they themselves affirmed what was known as "natural astrology" as a sound agricultural science. For clergy and laity, magic, supernatural powers, and spirit entities were very real, talismans and charms worked, and the question of whether something was acceptable or heretical came down to determining if the power/entity was from Satan or God. It is useful to remember that the Salem witchcraft trials did not end, in 1692, because participants decided there was no "real" evidence of deviltries, but rather because the judges became concerned that the appearance of harassing specters that looked like accused witches might actually be the Devil trying to get good people wrongly tried and convicted. In claiming that the supernatural is real and that they are working on the good side of the paranormal equation, and in utilizing rituals, incantations, tools, and manuals that look at times strikingly similar (if not identical) to those of their foes, Third Wave spiritual warfare authors look more familiar to students of American religious history than some might initially imagine.

CONCLUSION: EVERYTHING BLENDED

One focus of Third Wave manuals is demarcating the boundaries between the acceptable and unacceptable, the pure and impure. And, yet, the lines between what is acceptable and unacceptable are not always clear; at the edges of mission work, disagreements arise. As noted earlier, Third Wave writers such as Ed Murphy and F. Douglas Pennoyer suggest that some aspects of other peoples' cultures are fine, but some elements must be rejected as demonic. Spiritual warfare practitioners are aware that their own practices are occasionally labeled "syncretistic," one of the things Third Wave writers rail against as satanic. How the boundaries of "syncretism" are negotiated can be seen in Richard Twiss's 2003 book, *One Church Many Tribes: Following Jesus the Way God Made You*. As will be seen in the next chapter, Third Wave writers focus intensely on reconciliation with Native Americans. Twiss, an evangelical and Lakota Sioux who has connections to some Third Wave writers and shares some of their demonologies, writes, "I readily acknowledge that when attempting to redeem culture—sorting out the usable from the unusable—there is a need to be cautious so that we do not cross the line into syncretistic practices that combine idolatrous or occultic spiritual ceremonies with Christian ways and doctrines." At the same time, Twiss warns that he doesn't want "fleshly fear" to deter indigenous peoples from finding "a more native cultural expression of Christian faith."[60]

As an example of some things he considers acceptable, Twiss suggests that "many Christians would say that any Native who believes a tree can talk must be practicing animism, spiritism, or pantheism, although Jesus spoke directly to the winds and the waves and they heard him and obeyed." He later describes how the ritual of throwing horse milk to appease a mountain god can be adapted so that it is performed in gratitude to Jesus. "This is a classic example," he writes, "of how a cultural custom can be reinterpreted and redeemed from its former idolatrous usage and sanctified to express Christian faith, without disparaging Native culture." Interestingly, and despite positive blurbs from movement figureheads such as F. Douglas Pennoyer,

Peter Wagner, and Eddie Smith, many, if not most, spiritual warfare practitioners would find such activities and beliefs unacceptable. For example, someone I spoke with who engaged in a spiritual warfare "prayer walk" to discern demons told me that his group had discovered a "Native American spirit" in a tree on a public university campus in Michigan and proceeded to expel it with prayer and anointing oils. This person would assert that the spirits one might find in trees and winds are always (*especially* if related to Native Americans) demonic. And, while most spiritual warfare practitioners strongly agree with Twiss that the intention behind ritual actions is of prime importance, many would also suggest that some rituals and some material objects are "by nature" demonic. Twiss reveals his own assumptions about this when he describes the combination of Roman Catholic sacraments with Latin American indigenous practices to create "a very superstitious concoction."[61] Here, Twiss mirrors the Third Wave spiritual warfare movement as a whole: it draws boundaries that attack the syncretism and demonic status of other peoples' religions, cultures, and politics while simultaneously ignoring its own hybrid nature.

But this kind of strategy is not particular to this one group of demon-fighting evangelicals. Indeed, the Third Wave movement itself is attacked by other Christians—sometimes evangelical ones who practice different styles of spiritual warfare—as syncretistic in ways that similarly draws boundaries that cordon off their own traditions from criticism. The theologians Walter Wink and Michael Hardin, for example, refer to Wagner's "Strategic Level Spiritual Warfare" as nothing more than "archaic pagan religion dressed up as Christianity." The Calvinist David Powlison similarly asserts that Third Wave spiritual warfare has built its practical theology from "ingredients incompatible with our shared Christian faith."[62] There is nothing surprising in these accusations, and the assertion that Third Wave spiritual warfare is a syncretistic hybrid is correct. But in making these criticisms, apologists are using Wagner's version of spiritual warfare to draw a boundary of their own, arguing that their preferred form of Christianity is *not* just as "syncretistic" as the one they attack. Yet, if anything, the Third Wave's search for purification is only a more elaborate and endlessly fascinating version of what is done by any social formation we might label "religion": imagine itself whole, pure, original, and right. But the search for purity suggests that there is no such thing, that all is syncretistic, hybrid, combined, and merged.[63] Everything blended, though seldom recognized as such.

CHAPTER TWO

POSSESSED POSSESSIONS, DEFILED LAND, AND THE HORRORS OF HISTORY

Demonic spirits seem to crave a material presence.
Eddie and Alice Smith, *Spiritual Housecleaning*

Real demons do attach themselves to animals, idols, brass rings, trees, mountains, and buildings.
Harold Caballeros, *Victorious Warfare*

When I interviewed Mark, he was in his mid-twenties.[1] A recent college graduate, he had grown up the child of Third Wave intercessors. His father and mother were both recognized by the members of their church as particularly adept at spiritual warfare. Every weekday morning, in the car before dropping their son off at school, his parents would "pray the armor of God" (Ephesians 6: 10–20) over Mark to protect him from the demons lurking in the public building's hallways and textbooks. These Bible verses, used by Third Wave evangelicals as a protective prayer when fighting demons, urge the reader to put on the "belt of truth," "breastplate of righteousness," "helmet of salvation," and other warrior gear to protect oneself "against the powers of this dark world and against the spiritual forces of evil in the heavenly realm." On regular occasions, they would pray over Mark's toys and ask God to reveal if any had demonic inhabitants. On occasion, Mark said, the answer would be "yes," and they would stand above those specific toys, recite prayers, and then destroy and discard them. Mark said that when he left home for college, he eventually began to think

45

that his parents and church were wrong, that there weren't demons living in toys, harassing individuals, and lurking in public school textbooks. He told me that he didn't "believe" these things anymore. However, Mark said that, whenever he passed the horror aisle in a video store, his heart would race and he would feel the need to leave the area. While his thinking assured him that demons didn't reside in the movie boxes, his body—steeped for years in the Third Wave imaginary—anxiously behaved as if they did.

The majority of Americans might not share the Third Wave theology that objects and places can be possessed. But material possessions are an integral part of everyday life and identity. As the material-culture scholar Daniel Miller notes, "people sediment possessions, lay them down as foundations, material walls mortared with memory. . . ." And in the present postindustrial era (when consumer capitalism has become the primary driver of the US economy), the objects we possess and desire play an increasingly significant role in our attempts to establish a stable "self," a unique personality to portray and display. The late-modern notion of self, partly shaped by what Colin Campbell described as the co-emergence of "romanticism and the consumer ethic," appears (even when material, historical, and social realities suggest otherwise) not so much to be something dictated by one's family and career, but something fashioned over time, indeed continually being fashioned. Identity formation is a process, a flexible "project of the self." The sociologist Anthony Giddens argues that this structural compulsion to actively seek identities and lifestyles is "strongly influenced by the standardizing effects of commodity capitalism" and is thus "translated into one of the possession of desired goods and the pursuit of artificially framed lifestyles."[2] We are possessed by our possessions. We use them to shape our "selves" while they simultaneously create dissatisfactions and slot us into particular identities that mold our desires and actions.

In addition to their importance in the greater society, material items hold significance for Third Wave writers in their role as a conduit for "paramediation." The religious studies scholar Jeremy Biles has coined this term to describe objects "through which believers take themselves to be in the presence of something heterogeneous, paranormal, or deriving from the beyond."[3] In spiritual warfare, the things "deriving from beyond" are, of course, demons. These evil spirits reside in both objects and places, and Third Wave stories of possessed possessions and haunted land resemble the concepts and practices seen in contemporary ghost reality television. Programs such as *Possessed Possessions*, *The Haunted Collector*, *The Haunted*, *Paranormal State*, and *My Ghost Story Caught on Tape* feature haunted objects, houses, and land. As in tales found in spiritual warfare manuals, things and places are cursed. In addition, Third Wave literature and ghost reality television both prominently feature motifs of hauntings and curses related to Native Americans. As noted in the previous chapter, ghost reality television and Third Wave demonologies are deeply intertwined; they feed off each other and other cultural conduits in ways that make an academic quest for the origins of these motifs both difficult and irrelevant. Again, the apparent uniqueness that some students of American religion grant Third Wave evangelicalism, which both influences and is influenced by American supernatural narratives, is more an issue of scholarly dispositions, preferences, and classifications than empirical observation.

"Real demons," writes Harold Caballeros, "do attach themselves to animals, idols, brass rings, trees, mountains, and buildings as well as to any number and variety of manufactured and natural objects."[4] In this chapter, I examine the contours of the Third Wave imaginary's theology of possessed possessions and haunted places.

POSSESSED POSSESSIONS

Spiritual warfare manuals focused on sanctifying one's home and possessions describe a plethora of demon-inhabited objects. Two books in this genre are Eddie and Alice Smith's *Spiritual Housecleaning* and Chuck Pierce and Rebecca Systema Wagner's *Protecting Your Home from Spiritual Darkness*. The Smiths assert that "demonic spirits seem to crave a material presence," while practitioner Chuck Pierce writes that "there is often an invisible spiritual force behind a visible object."[5]

But the theme of possessed possessions is not relegated to just these specialty handbooks. In other works on spiritual warfare, for example, the intercessor Cindy Jacobs warns readers of the demonic dangers that can accompany antique furniture, and Harold Caballeros cautions his audience to be wary of purchasing statues while on missionary work in foreign lands.[6] In the academic study of religion, and as aptly critiqued by the material-religion scholar Amy Whitehead, "religious objects are largely relegated to being symbolic and representational instead of tangible, sensual, or embodied forms of religious expression." But material objects—as Whitehead and others have noted—are not just *reflections* of cultural values; they embody values in and of themselves.[7] And they don't just symbolize agency; at times—at least from the perspective of spiritual warfare's practitioners—they act as agents.

"Many of us are suffering today," the Smiths suggest, "because we have sometimes willfully, and sometimes ignorantly, invited possessions and behaviors into our homes that defile the atmosphere and give the devil the right to affect our lives and the lives of our children." Pierce writes that demons can gain access to objects, locations, and human bodies "through sin, trauma, victimization, witchcraft, occult practices or cursing."[8] In Third Wave literature, combined demonic desires for materiality and malfeasance lead to objects becoming possessed. When this occurs, material objects become demonic subjects that act in the human world. But it isn't just the cravings of evil spirits that cause such possessions. Human desires, family histories, and even the nature of a material object itself can lead to demonic habitation.

Throughout spiritual warfare manuals, the objects connected to an individual's extramarital affairs, pornography addictions, drug use, or occult practices house demons. As will be seen in chapter three, Third Wave theology asserts that one can even inherit demons from one's ancestors, and those demons can then come to inhabit certain possessions. And certain objects are, by their very nature, subject to possession by evil spirits. While the Smiths suggest that "most objects in the world are neither good nor evil in and of themselves," both they and Pierce provide lengthy lists of forbidden ones. These include "occult" materials such as Ouija boards and amulets, statues depicting divine figures from other religions such as Buddha or Greek deities, objects garnered from groups such as the Masons, Roman Catholic rosaries and crucifixes, popular-culture items such as Dungeons and Dragons or *Masters of the Universe* toys and games, and even "evil depictions of creatures such as lions, dogs, dragons or cats (or any other creature made with demonic distortions)."[9]

In addition to statues, non-evangelical religious objects, jewelry, and toys associated with the occult, spiritual warfare authors assert that demons can often be found in books (not their own, of course). The texts, illustrations, and subjects that volumes contain can invite demonic habitation. The Smiths relate one story of a family plagued by the presence of "spiritual entities roaming through their house at night." Upon investigating, the Smiths were informed through God-given discernment that something evil resided in the attic. Climbing through a garage ceiling entrance, the Smiths "discovered a large card-board box filled with Stephen King novels" that had been left by the previous owners. When the books were removed, the spirits disappeared. In another recollection, the Smiths tell about a haunting in their own Houston home. At times, the corner of their family room would be visited by an evil presence that was sometimes accompanied by a strange odor. One night, after again sensing the resident evil, the Smiths examined the objects in the afflicted corner. On the fireplace mantle sat what they described as an "elegant" and "beautifully bound" six-volume set of books they had inherited from a deceased aunt. Having never before opened the books, the Smiths were shocked to find "pages filled with lithographs of ghosts, gargoyles and grave-yards with spirits ascending from the tombstones." "After repenting to the Lord for allowing these books into our home," they write, "we spoke aloud, breaking any contracts with demons that were using the books as an access point into our home."[10] After this ritual, the books were discarded. The evil presence and its accompanying stench never reappeared.

Compact discs, like books, can house demons. In one story, Chuck Pierce tells of the time that his son bought the soundtrack to one of the Godzilla films. Hearing his son play a song from it, which Pierce considered "terrible," he tried discussing the lyrics with his son. When this conversation failed to convince the boy to get rid of the CD, Pierce prayed to God to "reveal the truth" behind it. "A few nights later he was visited by an evil, tangible presence," Pierce writes of his son, "the force was the same color as that on the soundtrack . . . he immediately confessed his sin to his mother and me and destroyed the CD."[11]

The destruction of the compact disc was an act of deliverance, which is the focus of spiritual warfare. Acts of deliverance can be performed on people, places, objects, and even regions or entire countries. The exorcism of demons from things frequently requires their destruction. Books, records, jewelry, statues, and clothing are burnt, smashed, and thrown away as final ritual actions following prayers of repentance for the sins that tied demons to the objects. In one story, Chuck Pierce tells how he was attached to the monetary value of his wife, Pam's, jewelry box, even though it was decorated with dragons, Buddhas, and pagodas. While Pam realized that these symbols made it a sinister demonic abode and wanted to destroy it, Chuck thought it was just too valuable, and disagreed. "My wife immediately submitted to me," Pierce writes, "and did not mention it anymore."[12]

But this act of wifely submission didn't end the matter. During a prayer meeting shortly after, God spoke directly to Pierce, saying "You have caused your wife to rebel against My will for her life, and I hold you accountable!" Pierce realized then that God wanted the jewelry box destroyed and decided that he must immediately do it. He got home, started a fire, and grabbed the box. "When I placed the jewelry box in the fireplace," Pierce writes, "a strange eerie wind began to blow and stir all around the living room." The wind, which he notes was generated from within the breezeless house, blew hard enough to knock a lamp down. Pierce called a church friend "who understood spiritual things," and "she told me to read some Scriptures and command any evil presence linked with that jewelry box to leave our home." Pierce continues, "when I did so, the Lord spoke to me and said, 'I am delivering you from covetousness and the love of money!'" With that, the wind died down and the ties that bound Pierce to covetous forces of habit began to wane. Thus, with the destruction of the jewelry box, a process of change began for Pierce, one in which "freedom began to come to us in incredible ways—not only freedom, but spiritual revelation."[13]

HAUNTED SPACES AND PLACES

In his 1999 how-to manual *Informed Intercession: Transforming Your Community Through Spiritual Mapping and Strategic Prayer*, George Otis Jr. describes the spiritual warfare being fought on earth today between demons and evangelicals by making references to World War I battlefields. Otis is one of the originators of the Third Wave evangelical practice known as "spiritual mapping," as well as the founder of the Sentinel Group, a Protestant research group based in Lynnwood, Washington. He tells readers that they need to enter and patrol the contested "no-man's land" that exists between the trenches of God's and Satan's armies. "If you want to obtain a good look at the enemy's deployments and deceptive weaponry in your community," Otis asserts, "you must be prepared to reconnoiter the front lines." "The focus of your observational patrols," he continues, "should be on places where enemy activity has assumed distinctive proportions and on human behaviors that offer evidence of demonic allegiances or a renewed hunger for godly values."[14] Otis is not writing metaphorically here. As already discussed, spiritual warfare entails fighting real demons who occupy physical spaces—including human bodies, objects, places of residence, tracts of land, and even entire cities and countries. Two spaces and places that garner a great deal of attention are "haunted houses" and "defiled land." These locations, in the Third Wave Evangelical imaginary, might be described as "spatial limbos," interstitial and contested no-man's lands in which the sins of history materialize in the form of demons. "Limbo" is an apt term, because, in general, Third Wave deliverance manuals reside in and engage with the spaces in between, that existing in the unmarked yet pregnant limbo amid various boundaries, including those between different religious expressions, acceptable and unacceptable desires, divine and human agency, and heresy and orthodoxy. In this section, I hope to "make material" Third Wave

Evangelical imaginings of physical space and their rituals to purify it, activities that might be described as attempts to fix the interstitial and vaguely bounded into position, to name it and claim for it a classification and moral assessment.

For Third Wave practioners, spaces, like objects, are filled with ghostly apparitions, foul odors, and shadowy figures. The cofounders of the Texas-based U.S. Prayer Center, Eddie and Alice Smith, speak for the movement as a whole when they write that they "firmly believe in haunted houses, haunted church buildings—even haunted hotels!" No place is safe. In what might be construed as an expansion of Jeffrey Sconce's notion of "haunted media" to "possessed technology," the Third Wave author Chuck Pierce describes a spirit-inhabited seminary apartment where the mircrowave beeped without explanation, the answering machine made strange noises, and lights turned on and off by themselves. But hauntings, according to Third Wave theology, never involve human spirits returned from the dead. As explained by Pierce, the seminary dorm "was not haunted by ghosts of human beings but rather by demonic forces whose job was to cloud the air with oppressive darkness."[15] In spiritual warfare manuals, haunted spaces are always demon-inhabited no-man's lands where evil spirits patrol and hope to control.

HAUNTED HOUSES: HAPPENSTANCE ENCOUNTERS WITH SINFUL PASTS

In *The Third Wave of the Holy Spirit*, Peter Wagner tells the story of his haunted Altadena, California, home. Wagner writes that he had no idea who had lived in the house previously or what events might have transpired there before his family took residence. They had lived in the sixty-year-old home for seventeen years without noticing anything unusual before two members of his Sunday school class, each of whom had the charismatic gift of discerning spirits, told him that there was something wrong. They went to the Wagners' bedroom to pray, which they did without incident. But "not long afterward, in the middle of the night when I was away," writes Wagner, "my wife Doris woke up with a terrible fear." She had awakened to see a figure with luminous green eyes standing in the corner of the bedroom. She "recognized that it was an evil spirit and rebuked it in the name of Jesus."[16] When Doris commanded the spirit to leave the house, the figure responded by moving back and forth and then disappearing.

After the two adult Sunday school students, George and Cathy, heard this story, they wanted to help. They visited the Wagners' home (by invitation) while the family was out. Upon arriving, the two could not get through the front door because of some unseen yet "powerful physical force resisting them." Choosing to instead go through the garage, they sensed strong energy, and "Cathy could actually smell the evil." She also noticed an ax on the wall that evoked in her a strong sense of past violence. Given such environmental cues, George and Cathy felt that they had discovered an evil spirit in the garage and proceeded to cast it out. They then entered the house and again "sensed the presence of evil." Noticing a stone puma on the living room table, which the Wagners had brought home from mission work in Bolivia, George sensed that the object was demon-inhabited and that its spirit was moving around the room. The two pursued the spirit until it left and then moved upstairs to the bedrooms. While they declared the daughter's room "relatively free of evil," both George and Cathy sensed a strong demonic presence in the Wagners' bedroom. Then "George saw a vision in the exact spot where my wife had seen the spirit," Wagner writes. "[I]t was a vivid scene of a man with an ax involved in great violence . . . in his spirit he heard a loud scream which appeared to come from a woman. . . . Whether a murder had been committed there or not, George could not be sure."[17] George and Cathy's work casting out these demons was apparently successful, as Wagner reports that the house has been "clean" of demons since.

In another story, Chuck Pierce tells of Elaine and her three-year-old son Joey, who had not slept soundly through a single night in the six months since they had moved into their house. Elaine called her pastor's wife, Joan, who suggested that they pray together in Joey's room. "As the women began praying," Pierce writes, "Joan had a strong sense that something in the room was truly wrong—that there was an evil presence there." She then began to get an image of a child being beaten in the room and "knew that the Lord was showing her why the evil presence lingered in Joey's room." Upon telling this to Elaine, the mother reported that Joey repeatedly awoke from nightmares in which he was being beaten by someone, though she assured Joan that neither she nor her husband had ever struck him "with force." Concluding that demons were present because of the sinful violence of past residents, Joan and Elaine prayed "to forgive the sin of child abuse that had taken place in the room." Both women cried as they identified with the suffering child who had once lived in the room. Joan then called upon God to cleanse the space, commanding the demon to leave the house and never return. "At that moment, a great peace descended upon the house," writes Pierce, "the room looked brighter," and Elaine "felt an inner peacefulness for the first time since moving in."[18]

In spiritual warfare manuals, as noted earlier, demons can appear as a result of personal sins and generational curses. In the first case, sinful individual choices invite spirits in; in the second, the wicked activities of one's ancestors have brought a family demon into being. But in the narratives about Peter Wagner's house and Joey's room, those who encounter evil spirits have not brought it upon themselves through sin, nor have they inherited it from their families. Rather, they are innocent victims who have unwittingly come to inhabit locations where the sins of past owners haunt the present. Recall that in Third Wave theology, human activities "invite" demons to physically reside in places. Thus, a site of murder, violence, domestic abuse, or occult activity becomes haunted by demons. The new human tenants find themselves in places of past sin and sorrow, locations where the violence and suffering that was repressed has disturbingly burst forth to torment them.

In *Spiritual Housecleaning*, the Smiths distinguish between demonic visitation and demonic habitation. They suggest that demons regularly visit and harass those who serve God as spiritual warfare soldiers. "In fact," they write, "if you plan to serve God on the front lines of Kingdom warfare, you are going to occasionally confront the enemy." They recount how, once, after an intense deliverance session with a young woman, they were awakened that night by pounding on their roof. "We weren't going to let the enemy intimidate us," they state, "we commanded the angry demons to shut up and leave us alone."[19]

The Smiths differentiate such occasional spirit visitations suffered by God's warriors from the phenomenon of demonic habitation, in which evil beings have been attracted to a place by the "sin of the previous" occupants. In these cases, "demons are assigned to, or have simply decided to dwell in, certain locations." Because of this, "houses, graveyards, 'sacred' groves or places deemed by New Agers or witches to have special powers or which have been dedicated to demons may at times require deliverance counseling." The Smiths suggest numerous signs that a place may be demon-inhabited. Their list of thirteen symptoms of "defiled land" includes restless children, the appearance of ghosts and poltergeists, foul odors, insomnia, bad dreams, domestic arguments, and an "atmospheric heaviness, making it hard to breathe." Co-authors Chuck Pierce and Rebecca Systema Wagner reprint and cite the Smith's list in their own manual, suggesting that "if you are experiencing any of these things on an ongoing basis, ask the Lord to reveal any spiritual darkness that may be in your home."[20]

DEFILED LAND AND THE HORRORS OF HISTORY

Third Wave literature reveals houses and buildings haunted by demonic specters, evil spirits that have been conjured by the sinful actions of people who once lived there. In such tales, Third Wave demon hunters encounter a baby's room filled with three demons brought on by past child abuse, they investigate a haunted hotel made so by hosting a Haitian voodoo conference, and they battle evil in a house that won't sell because the past owners painted satanic symbols inside of it. But cases of spatial demonization extend even beyond buildings, to the ground itself. "Sin," writes Chuck Pierce, "produces a curse in the land—in the physical ground where it occurs—and where there are curses, evil abounds." Indeed, "just as the enemy can gain a foothold into our lives through sin, he also can gain a foothold into land through sin that has been committed there." This is so much the case that "the actual land can grieve once a sin is committed upon the ground."²¹ In other words, the land itself is haunted. It mourns due to past sins and sorrows. And where there are ghosts (who in the Third Wave imaginary are, of course, always demons), there is unfinished business.

Land defilement can occur through an individual's sins, and Third Wave lists of these sins include idolatry, bloodshed, immorality, and covenant breaking. On occasion, defilement occurs through sins of deception, as in the case—related by the Smiths—in which a land developer sold a plot to a congregation without telling them that it was a former Native American burial ground. The narrative, which sounds eerily similar to some motifs found in the popular 1982 film *Poltergeist*, has a theatrically dramatic quality that is common to most Third Wave demonization tales. The church built on the burial site was plagued with problems that included a bad escrow account, "putrid odors," and behavioral problems among the parishioners. These troubles continued and compounded until the entire church building was violently swept away by the San Jacinto River in a violent flood.²² But other narratives of demon habitation concern sins that are not just individual, but corporate, in nature. In these stories, the evil spirits that haunt the land have been summoned by the violence that has been committed by one group against another through colonization, enslavement, war, or genocide.

The Spiritual Warfare Network pastor Bob Beckett relates a story of defiled land haunted by the horrors of history in Southern California. In 1974, Beckett and his wife were asked to direct a minimum security juvenile facility owned by a church. Planted in the isolated desert community of San Jacinto, Beckett wondered "why the Lord would move us into the middle of nowhere." "Little did I know at the time," he adds, "that I had moved into a stronghold of darkness for a major portion of the Southern California Inland Empire!" Beckett discovered that the facility and its surroundings had a troubled past—particularly from a Third Wave evangelical perspective. The building itself had once been a Transcendental Meditation training center, while a Native American reservation nearby housed shamans, and another locality featured a natural site deemed by "New Agers" and others to be a sacred "navel" or "vortex" of the earth. More research uncovered a local history of tragedy, particularly violent human relationships that had resulted in curses and negative spiritual energies that blanketed the land with darkness. Nearby "Massacre Canyon," for example, was the site of the annihilation of one First Nation tribe by another. On the other side of the valley, a water company had flooded the land, leading to the loss of Native property and life. "Many on the reservation today can still recall how infuriated the tribal council became over this," Beckett writes. "[T]heir shamans cursed the white man's water company for their error."[23]

To combat the dark forces ruling over the land, God provided Beckett with a vision of a form, which looked like a bear hide, sporting claws and a large backbone. "Each time I would see the hide," writes Beckett, "it would be centered over our local mountain area." This vision spurred him to take twelve church leaders to an isolated cabin in the mountains. "We were to pray there," he writes, "until we broke the 'backbone' of this ruling spirit and forced it to loose its spiritual grip upon the people living under its control." Beckett's group arrived at the cabin and began hours of "praying and agonizing and ministering to the Lord." The thirteen members of the group began to feel surrounded by a sense of evil and responded by spontaneously singing the hymn, "There is Power in the Blood." The song banished the feeling of evil, even literally breaking the bear-hide demon's back. "Many of us even heard an audible sound as if vertebrae were not exactly cracking, but popping or disjointing," writes Beckett. "[T]he whole cabin physically shook!"[24] Following the experience, Beckett reported that positive "spiritual" things began to happen in the community.

Native Americans play a prominent role in defiled land narratives. By incorporating North America's indigenous peoples into their stories, Third Wave evangelicals follow in a long line of writers and movements in American history. Many scholars of American religion and culture have noted that Native American *spirits*, in particular, have appeared in a wide range of narratives: political writings, novels and short stories, and spiritualist séances.[25] In the spiritual warfare handbooks under study, Native Americans serve two complementary roles in the development of demon-haunted territories. First, as people who are presumed not to be evangelical Christians, they are perceived as in cahoots with the Devil and his demonic hordes. Thus, indigenous religiosity itself causes demonic infestation. Second, the exploitation and violence perpetrated by white European colonizers against Native Americans has also resulted in demonic presence. In other words, the sinful activities committed by whites *against* First Nation peoples have "invited" demons to defile the land as much as indigenous religions have. When Chuck Pierce offers instructions to readers who wish to research the past history of the land to find acts of individual and corporate sin that may have invited evil spirits to take up residence, he begins with two questions: "Who originally owned the land? Was it part of a broken treaty with Native Americans?"[26]

The ground grieves because of past sins committed upon it, and demons haunt the territory where such horrors occurred. In Third Wave literature, water, not just land, can grieve and house angry spirits brought on by past tragedy. The Bermuda Triangle is the section of the Atlantic Ocean made famous by media depictions of it as a mysterious, dangerous—even occult—limbo where ships, planes, and people disappear without a trace. While popular explanations of the Bermuda Triangle have ranged from alien abductions to kidnappers from Atlantis, the body of water appears in one of Peter Wagner's essays as a place demonized by past injustice. The Third Wave founder recounts the story of missionaries Kenneth McAll and his spouse, who, in 1972, became lost in a storm while sailing in the Bermuda Triangle. After they were rescued, McAll decided to research the area in hopes of finding the reason for so many mysterious accidents and disappearances. His investigation uncovered a shocking crime. Specifically, McAll came to believe that "in the Bermuda Triangle area the slave traders of a bygone day, in order to collect insurance, had thrown overboard some two million slaves who were too sick or weak to be sold" Convinced that the drowning murders of millions of enslaved Africans were the cause of the numerous sea and air tragedies—or, put more precisely, the Triangle's culprits were the demons who had been "invited" to inhabit the region by the combination of the slave traders' sins and the slaves' pagan religion—McAll felt God moving him to act. In July 1977, he organized a "Jubilee Eucharist" celebration in Bermuda. "The stated purpose was to seek 'the specific release of all those who had met their untimely deaths in the Bermuda Triangle.'" While the actual ritual is not described in any detail, it most likely included an intercessory prayer in which the participants prayed for forgiveness in the name of the slave traders and also for the souls of the deceased (and, it is assumed, non-Christian) African slaves. Regardless of its specific form, Wagner writes that the ritual was a success. "As a result the curse was lifted," he asserts, and "McAll reports that 'from the time of the Jubilee Eucharist until now . . . no known inexplicable accidents have occurred in the Bermuda Triangle.'"[27]

"If ghosts do not return to reveal crimes that have gone unpunished," writes the scholar Jeffrey Weinstock, "then evil acts may in fact go unredressed."[28] In spiritual warfare manuals, the land is not just haunted, but demon-infested, by past injustices, and it cries out for repentance. The Bermuda Triangle is haunted by the murder of slaves, while a Southern California desert is demonized by wars, man-made tragedies such as floods, and non-Christian (and thus, in the Third Wave view, satanic) religions such as Transcendental Meditation and Native American practices. And even more troubling than the fact of haunting is the fact that the ghosts of the past that are the demons of the present can also cause physical and spiritual harm. Planes and ships disappear; souls are lost at sea *and* from God's grace. In Third Wave literature, fruitless evangelizing, economic woes, and high crime are signs that a place is haunted by unfinished business. Action must be taken, demonic backbones must be broken. The spiritual warfare specialist Kjell Sjoberg performs ritual prayers to break the mental bonds of slavery in Africa, which, he argues, keep the Gospel from being heard, while the intercessor Cindy Jacobs prays for forgiveness for World War II Japanese internment camps with the hope that it might help banish the demons keeping God's message from being heeded in Japan.[29] The places of past tragedy become places of religious significance, where Satan's demons and God's warriors battle for the land and its inhabitants.

The ground that holds religious import is always a site of contestation where comfortable centers can't be found. Places of significance, to use the geographer Tim Cresswell's words, are locations that do "not have meanings that are natural and obvious but ones that are created by some people with more power than others to define what is and what is not appropriate."[30] But the desires of those with more power never fully control the meaning of a location, because spaces hold a multiplicity of contradictory meanings. Take, for example, Mount Rushmore in the Black Hills of South Dakota. As homage to US presidents, it might on the one hand be considered a sacred site of American civil religion. At the same time, though, it is a monument intentionally carved into a place that is sacred to the Lakota tribe, and thus is a landmark signifying the colonization and genocide of First Nation peoples by Europeans. After all, the Lakota were the Native Americans who defeated General Custer's army, the First Nation that most vehemently resisted forced removal to reservations, and the bulk of the nearly 300 individuals massacred at Wounded Knee in 1890. There is even a third persuasive interpretation of the place's continuing relevance for Lakota ethnic and locative identity that recognizes its ritual and community importance that preceded Mount Rushmore. No single, uncontested, meaning exists. "To make sense of Mt Rushmore's status as a sacred mountain within the context of the Black Hills as a whole," writes historian Matthew Glass, "it is necessary to acknowledge that the most vexing issue will likely be the multiplicity of interpretations and outright conflicts over the mountain's symbolic definition."[31]

In spiritual warfare manuals, too, the land holds multiple and conflicting meanings. The place in which a Christian nation triumphed over a non-Christian one may mark where the possibility of spreading the Gospel and saving souls began, but it is also likely the site of great violence perpetrated in the name of God and country. While the popular stereotype of theologically conservative evangelicals suggests unquestioning patriotism, Third Wave literature suggests that such a view can in some cases be much too simplistic. In spiritual warfare manuals, the patriotic narratives that whitewash American history of past violence and injustice are contested by the appearance of spirits, demons who erupt onto the scene and expose that which had been repressed in the "official" story. But, while such Third Wave "ghost stories" contest conservative historical revisionism, they should not be construed as intentional critiques of American imperialism. Rather, they are ambivalent legends, warning readers that history—whether individual or corporate—can never be forgotten. Indeed, we must often repent for it.

DELIVERING HOUSE AND LAND

For Pierce, as for all those Third Wave evangelicals at work banishing demons, some curios of one's individual, familial, or corporate past are best discarded. "In reality," writes Pierce, "the heirloom is not maintaining a link to their dead loved one but rather to a familial spirit who enjoys access to their homes through deception." Instead of keeping such ties to the past—and thus retaining demon infestation—the spiritual warfare practitioner must break the ties that bind. "Do we have a greater responsibility to honor past generations or to mold new ones?" asks Pierce.[32] As will be noted in further detail in the next chapter, Third Wave evangelicals thus stand in the space between modern and late-modern identities. As moderns, they recognize the self as inherently tied to family, community, and place. But, as late moderns, they insist on the possibility of loosening those ascribed identities and forming new ones. It is the need to fight against and ultimately banish the horrors of history that brought about the presence of demons that spiritual warfare manuals address. As "how-to" manuals of spiritual transformation, these handbooks provide rituals for expelling demons and repenting the past.

Demonized places, like demonized people and objects, need deliverance. While the ritual structure is similar to the one used for the deliverance of people, when dealing with places demonized by past tragedies and injustices, spiritual warfare practitioners are required to repent for others. This is referred to as "identificational repentance." "Even though you may not have been the one who committed the sin," writes Chuck Pierce, "you can go to God on behalf of whoever committed the sin and ask Him to forgive that sin and apply the blood of

Jesus to the land." Kenneth McAll's ritual jubilee for the historical horrors of the Bermuda Triangle and Kjell Sjoberg's prayer of repentance for West African slavery are two examples. The Smiths note that this even works for less dramatic sins, such as failing to keep up with house payments. In one story, the Smiths' acquaintances became financially troubled as soon as they took ownership of a home that had been foreclosed on. "When they repented to God for the financial sins of the previous owners, breaking any curses on the property and consecrating it to the Lord," they write, "they experienced an immediate financial breakthrough." The Smiths relate a similar success in selling a house that had been on the market for a long time when the current owners repented for previous owners' occult activities. In yet another example, the Smiths banished bad luck (and its accompanying demons) from a hotel after ritually repenting for a Haitian voodoo conference that had taken place in its rented ballroom.[33] Identificational repentance helps free places of their haunting pasts by having the spiritual warrior step in and seek forgiveness for the actions that originally invited the demons to reside there.

One might note here that the sins related to foreclosure are interpreted by the writers as being entirely those of the individual owners, not of a corporation that may have loaned to unqualified applicants or charged exceedingly high interest rates. Third Wave evangelicalism—just as neo-Pentecostalism and other forms of evangelicalism—tends to "individualize" problems to the extent that social sources, institutions, and forces that might be implicated in misfortune and injustice are ignored (more on this in chapter four).[34] In this sense, Third Wave theology offers what might be described as a "supernatural" hermeneutics of suspicion that contests the materialist hermeneutics of suspicion proposed by Marxism. In other words, in the place of social inequalities and laissez-faire neoliberal markets, the Third Wave imaginary conjures demons—summoned by the sins of individuals or groups—to explain social problems.

When one engages in rituals to deliver the land from demons, one also performs the act of consecrating the land for Christ. In addition to the previously described "prayerwalk," consecration can also take the form of the ritual of "staking the land" with wooden posts that have Bible verses written on them. This, in Pierce's words, gives one "the legal right and authority to declare the manifold wisdom of God to any evil force that crosses those boundaries." For example, the spiritual mapper Bob Beckett felt moved by God to place stakes in the ground around the small town of Hemet "in order to secure the spiritual canopy He wanted spread over the city." Heeding God's call, he collected both church elders and two-by-two oak stakes with "Isaiah 33:20–24" written on them. These verses include the lines "thine eyes shall see Jerusalem a quiet habitation, a tabernacle that shall not be taken down; not one of the stakes thereof shall ever be removed, neither shall any of the cords thereof be broken," and "the people that dwell therein shall be forgiven their iniquity." "At precisely 5:00 P.M.," writes Beckett, "each elder would drive his stake into the ground as a memorial unto the Lord, and the resulting canopy of prayer would remain as our declaration of strategic intercessory warfare against the encroaching darkness." Similarly, Chuck Pierce describes how—when moving into a new house in Colorado Springs, Colorado—he invited thirty friends over, took four oak stakes with Bible verses written in marker on each side, and handed them out to the group. "Teams of about four or five then went to each corner of the property," Pierce writes, "read the Scriptures listed on their stakes, prayed a prayer of blessing and consecration, and then drove their stake into the ground using a sledgehammer." Pierce mentions five specific scriptures on the stakes, including Psalm 91, which describes the Lord as a "refuge and fortress" and states that there is no need for fear, assuring that "neither shall any plague come nigh thy dwelling."[35] The other verses were Isaiah 54:2–3, Jeremiah 29:7, Luke 1:37, and Joshua 24:15. After staking the land, they went into the house and "raised a canopy of praise" through song and worship.

CONCLUSION: THE SPATIAL LIMBOS OF SPIRITUAL WARFARE

Scholars of religious studies have long examined "sacred spaces" as sites of religious significance. For those influenced by one of the field's founding fathers, Mircea Eliade, sacred space might be conceived as that location housing cosmic order and meaning, as opposed to chaos and meaninglessness—"place" as opposed to "placelessness," to use E. C. Relph's phrasing—a "home" that exists as an "irreplaceable centre of significance."[36] According to such conceptions, sites such as mountains and waterfalls may become *axis mundi*, topophilic (literally loved) places where the humanist geographer Yi Fu Tuan imagines a significant affective bond of meaning is established between place and people.[37] But in spiritual warfare manuals, places such as homes, neighborhoods, towns, regions, mountains, valleys, and bodies of water are sites of religious contestation that are not *spaces* (meaning here unsignified territory), nor are they necessarily *topophilic* places that provide succor and security. Instead, they might be thought of as *spatial limbos*.

The popular employment of the term "limbo" utilizes its meaning as a state of being nowhere, existing in some unknown and undesired place or situation, or living in a state of aimlessness. But a perusal of the *Oxford English Dictionary* suggests another definition, one drawn from medieval Catholicism. According to this definition, limbo is also a "region supposed to exist on the border of Hell as the abode of the just who died before Christ's coming, and of unbaptized infants." Third Wave Evangelicals do not literally call the haunted houses and territories in which they battle Satan's demons "limbos," nor do they have such a theological concept in which to locate the unsaved that were made so by misfortunes of ancient birth or untimely death. Indeed, its origins in medieval Catholicism would likely make the notion anathema to these conservative Protestants, heirs to the Reformation that fought against such doctrines. But spiritual warfare's evil spirits, conjured by past injustices and the lost souls they represent, evoke a location betwixt and between the angelic and the demonic, between heaven and hell. Such sites are spiritual battlefields that, far from being empty, are overdetermined with ambivalent meaning and significance.

CHAPTER THREE

THE GOTHIC THERAPEUTIC

If you choose to live a glass-half-empty life, you are doomed to disillusionment. The natural law of attraction guarantees it.
Alice Smith, *Beyond the Lie*

Damaged, demonized adults tend to raise damaged, demonized children and grandchildren.
Ed Murphy, *The Handbook of Spiritual Warfare*

The late-modern present is filled with what Anthony Giddens refers to as "projects of the self." In his interpretation, and noted at beginning of the last chapter, we live in a time in which we are propelled by forces beyond our control to seek out stable and satisfying identities. With this can come the desire for some sort of dramatic personal change, an explosive catharsis that destroys what was once there. While "catharsis" might not exactly be everyday parlance for working on one's self, the idea that one should engage in such labor is central to modern life. Terms and idioms such as change, transformation, self-improvement, nurturing emotional well-being, finding one's "true" self, and building self-esteem are commonplace phrases, activities, and desires that register the visibility and power of therapeutic discourse in contemporary American culture. The reverberations of the therapeutic can be seen throughout the media landscape. Bestseller lists from the 1950s to the present provide a plethora of self-help manuals that tout how the "power of positive thinking," "the seven habits of highly effective people," or taking "the road less traveled" can help you "live your best life now." Media icon Oprah Winfrey—through her television channel, website, and publishing empire—specializes in providing tips to aid self-transformation. Even television mobster Tony Soprano explored his anger issues on a therapist's couch. But these are just a couple of the more visible examples of a much larger cultural ethos. Therapeutic discourse offers pre-scripted life narratives of vulnerability, trauma, and triumph through continuous programs of self-improvement. "From birth, to marriage and parenting, through to bereavement, people's experience is interpreted through the medium of the therapeutic ethos," writes Frank Furedi. The social theorist Eva Illouz further argues that therapeutic discourse is so commonplace and habitual that "it is now virtually impossible to isolate this language from other 'master cultural' codes such as that of economic liberalism or contractual law."[1]

Therapeutic discourse resonates thoroughly within the actors, habits, and institutions of the neoliberal era. As a result, it is no surprise that Third Wave spiritual warfare literature—specifically deliverance manuals that teach readers how to banish tormenting demons—frequently reproduce the language and structures of therapeutic discourse as it is found in self-help literature. The concern with the effects of past and present trauma, as well as the healing powers of positive thinking, also appear with some frequency in Third Wave manuals. Yet, this is therapeutic discourse with a markedly darker tone than that found in an issue of O: The Oprah Magazine or the latest bestseller by Dr. Phil.[2] In this chapter, I argue that Third Wave writings—particularly self-help deliverance manuals that teach readers how to expel demons from oneself and others—comprise a distinctly Gothic therapeutic in which the trope of haunting is used to evoke and explain the negative influence of past trauma and sin in one's present life.

In a technical sense, "Gothic" and "therapeutic" may seem irreconcilable. After all, the term "Gothic" conjures the grotesque, the decaying, and the repressed. One imagines dilapidated castles, hauntings, and hopeless yearning. "Therapeutic," on the other hand, evokes healing, growth, and purification. No dark shadows or suppressed secrets there. Yet, individual deliverance stories in spiritual warfare manuals simulate both of these languages. Even more, Third Wave handbooks *merge* them in unique ways, enabling these tropes to take new shapes and assume new directions. The old languages are transformed into the hybrid I call the Gothic therapeutic.

I am struck by how spiritual warfare's demons—like ghosts—haunt the present because of what has happened in the past. And this is not metaphorical—at least not for the authors under discussion. It must be remembered that for Third Wave evangelicals, demons are actual entities. They work on earth to do Satan's bidding and are part of what the evangelical missionary Paul Hiebert dubbed the "excluded middle," those superhuman and supernatural forces that exist in the limbo between the cosmic and earthly realms.[3] But in the narratives offered by deliverance manuals, demons are also what I will describe as "forces of habit" generated by past sinful acts and family history. When Third Wave writers discuss demons, they are—to quote the deliverance minister and emeritus Fuller Seminary professor Charles Kraft—"talking about control over people and their habits."[4] A person's sinful past activities, the generational curses that he has inherited, and the traumatic experiences that he has had create "openings" and "invitations" that allow demons to enter his body and influence his thoughts. The unique Third Wave rituals of demonic deliverance—spirit binding, prayers of repentance, object destruction, and other activities—then, are methods for banishing demons *and* breaking historically inculcated forces of habit. In effect, the deliverances (Third Wave for "exorcism") of spiritual warfare—which occur in both living rooms and church auditoriums—function for practitioners as a Gothic therapeutic that seeks to banish what was once repressed, but is now a returning past.

In this chapter, I do several things. I first point to the shared idioms between Third Wave manuals and the larger genre of self-help literature. Second, I briefly place the movement's conceptions of haunting and demons into conversation with the growing scholarship on ghosts and the supernatural in American culture. I then move on to examine the ways in which Third Wave handbooks assert how people can become demonized, discuss spiritual warfare rituals to expel demons, and consider how deliverance narratives constitute a discourse about human agency that wavers between choice and imposition. I conclude the chapter by discussing how some concepts and understandings of demonization, such as "generational inheritance," rely upon the notion of a socially located and historically constituted individual that is very different from the autonomous and independent one posited by the neoliberal imaginary.

THIRD WAVE DELIVERANCE MANUALS AND THERAPEUTIC DISCOURSE

Journalists, American religion scholars, and others who have examined Third Wave evangelicalism are understandably struck by how different its world of demons, prayer warriors, and spiritual mapping appears when compared to the broader currents of contemporary American culture. Spiritual warfare's prominent Manichean dualism of good and evil—mixed in with its martial terminology of battles, trenches, bombs, and warfare—seems especially distant from the therapeutic, positive-thinking, and self-help language of figures such as Joel Osteen, Oprah Winfrey, and Marianne Williamson. Some Third Wave writers even explicitly attack what they refer to as "pop psychology" and the "culture of victimhood."[5] But a closer look suggests that these writers use therapeutic language in ways that are at times nearly indistinguishable from the larger self-help genre.

Several writers replicate the words and phrases prominent in therapeutic discourse. Eddie Smith tells readers in his deliverance manual, *Breaking the Enemy's Grip*, that "there are simply no shortcuts to spiritual adulthood" and features sections with titles such as "installing love." In her manual on how to keep demons from harassing your children, Rebecca Greenwood includes sections on "inner healing" and urges us to turn our child's "I can't" into "I can."[6] While, understandably, Christian references appear more frequently in spiritual warfare manuals than in some self-help literature (such as when Eddie Smith tells readers that "Dr. Jesus' prescription for the healing of your wounded heart calls for regular applications of love and prayer over an extended period of time"), the pop psychology terms and phrases are often the same.

In addition to language and phrasing, Third Wave manuals share with self-help literature a penchant for lists. Steps to forgiving, stages of Christian living, paths to freedom, and innumerable other numbered points and bullets make up significant portions of some guides. The writer Alice Smith even reproduces *Purpose Driven Life* author Rick Warren's list of "eight principles for living a victorious life in Christ," complete with the handy acronym "RECOVERY." Many spiritual warfare manuals include self-assessment documents, often in an appendix, that will help the reader figure out whether they are demonized and what other personal spiritual issues they might need to work on. Some of these documents take the form of quizzes in which each answer garners points, resulting in a sum that can be understood through a grading key provided by the author. Discussing this element in Guatemalan neo-Pentecostal literature, the anthropologist Kevin Lewis O'Neill writes that such "numbers signal a melding of logics, teaching each neo-Pentecostal how to manage himself or herself as well as to see the most intangible qualities as quantifiable."[7] The "quantifiability of the unquantifiable" and the production of lists are ways that Third Wave manuals conform to contemporary therapeutic discourse.

While the genre of self-help literature is large and varied, one recurrent strain touts the power of positive mental attitude for success, wealth, health, and emotional well-being. Since the mid-to-late nineteenth century, a variety of religious movements and figures have asserted the power of mind over matter, will over historical and material circumstance. These include Phineas Parkhurst Quimby and Mesmerism, Mary Baker Eddy and Christian Science, the varieties of New Thought, Father Divine and his Peace Mission Movement, Norman Vincent Peale, Robert Schuller, New Age spirit channels such as J. Z. Knight/Ramtha, and the prosperity gospel of the Word of Faith Movement.[8] Think positively, the spiel goes, and great things will come to you. But, think negatively, and you will suffer sickness, poverty, and spiritual darkness. A prominent example from the late 2000s was television writer/producer Rhonda Byrne's book on the "law of attraction" called *The Secret*. In February 2007, Oprah Winfrey devoted two episodes of her daytime talk show to Byrne's book and related video. Winfrey's promotion of books and authors has frequently resulted in sales boosts. Her embrace of *The Secret* proved no exception. By late March, the book dotted bestseller lists, and 3.75 million copies were in print.[9] In the small volume, Byrne touted the power of positive thinking, saying that a cosmic law of attraction worked such that positive thoughts would bring positive results. Ask, believe, and you shall receive. If you don't get it—whether the "it" is happiness, health, wealth, or love—it must at some level be your fault. Maybe negative thoughts have crept into your mind, maybe you just aren't spiritually ready for it now. The notion that one can think their way to the things they desire most—a historical discourse of which *The Secret* is just one recent iteration—is a prominent idiom of much self-help literature and practice.

Positive thinking and the power of willed belief to effect change register strongly in the deliverance manuals of several Third Wave authors. Rebecca Greenwood, for example, refers to negative feelings as "ungodly thought patterns," touts the "power of affirmation," and tells readers that their children can "pollute themselves or cause beautiful life by their thought patterns and spoken words."[10] Despite the fact that works such as *The Secret* and movements such as New Thought and Christian Science are considered satanic within the Third Wave community, reference to the "law of attraction" still makes an appearance in author Alice Smith's *Beyond the Lie: Finding Freedom from the Past*:

> If you choose to live a glass-half-empty life, you are doomed to disillusionment. The natural law of attraction guarantees it. You find in life what you are looking for, not what you are looking at. If your perspective on life, including your past, is miserable, you will stay miserable. It's all about your perception.

Smith continues by telling readers that "ten percent of what makes you who you are is what's happened to you" and "ninety percent of what makes you who you are is how you've chosen to respond to what's happened to you." While the figures and movements that tout the law of attraction might be defined as demonic by Smith, she and other Third Wave writers mine from the same grotto when they assert that ideas and consciousness come before materiality, belief comes before action, and "what you think determines your actions, your speech, and eventually your health."[11]

In addition to words, phrases, lists, and the power of positive attitudes, Third Wave manuals are filled with stories of traumatization, and trauma is the essential base upon which therapeutic discourse rests. The social theorist Eva Illouz argues that the "narrative of self-help is fundamentally sustained by a narrative of suffering."[12] In other words, the discourse of therapeutic self-help posits that normal human development inevitably involves traumatic negative events—experienced from infancy to adulthood—that make individuals dysfunctional. If they want to live up to their full potential in the boardroom and bedroom, they must overcome those traumas. In Third Wave manuals, trauma may come from childhood abuse, accidents, bullying, unemployment, and a host of other negative experiences.[13] Trauma is viewed as an event that "opens the door" to the possibility that the individual, in her sadness and oppression, will be receptive to the temptations of Satan and the indwelling of demons. Third Wave traumatization tropes frequently involve stories about demon-haunted adults who suffered physical and/or sexual abuse as children. Sometimes, the story is the author's own. In *Beyond the Lie*, author Alice Smith relates her history of being sexually abused as a six-year-old, stalked by a predatory male at twelve, nearly raped at seventeen, and harassed by a peeping Tom at eighteen.[14]

Because it is considered a universal human experience within therapeutic discourse and Third Wave theology, trauma's meaning is broadened in the latter case to include a variety of negative events. For example, Rebecca Greenwood relates the story of Betty, who becomes demonized after suffering the trauma of her alcoholic father forgetting to take her to her birthday pizza party. In another work, Greenwood writes about Daniel, who as a teen was so traumatized by loneliness and lack of friends that he eventually became what she describes as a "full blown Satanist." In deliverance manuals, people who were not even born when the traumatic event occurred still suffer the effects of the traumas experienced by their parents, whose negative emotions redound on their children. This is especially the case when the conception takes place out of wedlock, during violent sex, a rape, or in which the couple harbored negative thoughts during the sexual act. Greenwood writes that "trauma even at the moment of conception, throughout the pregnancy, and during childhood can lead a person into rejection and rebellion."[15]

Within therapeutic discourse, the individual's main task is to bring her traumatic experiences to consciousness and, in effect, render them powerless through recognition. "The narrative of self-help and self-realization is a narrative of memory and memory of suffering," writes Illouz, "but it is simultaneously a narrative in which the exercise of memory brings redemption from it."[16] Third Wave writers mirror this trope. "Once the door of victimization and trauma is open in your life," writes Alice Smith, "it remains until you (the victim) slam it shut." Deliverance manuals suggest that closing the door of victimization means that one must recognize her past traumas and develop an attitude of forgiveness in order to banish the demons that torment her. Several Third Wave writers additionally stress that forgiveness is the most important part of the process and that God becomes angry with those who cannot enact it. Eddie Smith, for example, asserts that when we refuse to forgive, God will "release us to demonic tormentors for discipline until we learn to repent and forgive even as we have been forgiven." But, even more, Smith suggests, God may actually kill those who persist in their unwillingness to forgive. Sharing the story of an unforgiving man named "Pastor Jim," who died after refusing to heed multiple divine warnings, Smith tells readers that if we ignore God's demand that we forgive, "He may have no choice but to call us home."[17]

Eva Illouz suggests that the modern therapeutic view of mental health might be described as a "demonic narrative" in which trauma results from "the crises inherent in the very experience of living." Illouz explains that "a demonic narrative situates the source of suffering in an evil principle that is outside the subject, whether Satan or a traumatic event," and that "this form of evil is characterized by its ability to insidiously get inside the person."[18] Without a doubt, the spiritual warfare deliverance manuals under discussion register therapeutic discourse in a way that materializes the demonic narrative that Illouz describes. In the Third Wave imaginary, as illustrated by the words of Alice Smith, there are two different "victim spirits" involved in trauma cases. The first is the human being who has been violated and has embraced a "victim mindset" that "keeps the victimization pattern recurring, unless, or until, it's broken." The second, though, is not human, but "any one of a host of unseen demonic spirits who are attracted to and desire to attach themselves to a person who will embrace their lies and behaviors, accepting a victim identity." In other words, trauma weakens an individual's defenses and opens him up to demons, who then proceed to inhabit his body, torment his mind, and inhibit his functioning in everyday life. This is an existence in which "an unseen world of darkness filled with spirit beings is looking for an opportunity to harass and torment you."[19] Spiritual warfare deliverance manuals mirror the modern therapeutic discourse, but with a twist. Rather than basking in the light of therapeutic quick fixes, Third Wave literature lingers in the dark and decayed realm of the Gothic, demonizing inappropriate emotions, desires, activities, and cultural materials.

HAUNTING AS A GOTHIC TROPE IN AMERICAN CULTURE AND SCHOLARSHIP

One way to analyze Third Wave deliverance manuals is through the Gothic trope of haunting. In suggesting this, I am indebted to American religion and culture scholars such as Edward Ingebretson and Jason Bivins, who have elaborated on ways that we are living in what might be described as a haunted present.[20] Americans continue to be fascinated and tormented by supernatural entities. As recently noted by the scholar Jeffrey Weinstock, "our contemporary moment is a haunted one."[21] Television offerings suggest a consistency of interest over time, as reality programs such as *Ghost Hunters*, *Paranormal*

State, and *Ghost Adventures* have replaced dramas from the 1990s such as *Touched by an Angel* and *The X-Files*. Polls concur in suggesting a fascination with things that go bump in the night. A 2007 Pew Poll suggested that a majority of Americans believe that angels and demons roam the earth. In December 2009, Pew found that 29 percent of those asked "say they have felt in touch with someone who has recently died," while "almost one-in-five say they have seen or been in the presence of ghosts." Other polling organizations concur with Pew: a 2005 Gallup Poll found that 37 percent of Americans believe in haunted houses, and a 2005 CBS News Poll suggested that 48 percent of Americans believed in ghosts.[22]

While these numbers suggest that some Americans think they are haunted by supernatural beings, how might such entities be understood? In the last fifteen years, scholars have interpreted Americans' interests in angels, ghosts, and demons in a wide variety of ways. In addressing what he saw as the growing interest in angels and the supernatural in the 1980s and 1990s, for example, the sociologist Robert Wuthnow pondered whether such interests were "probably symptomatic of the growing uncertainty many people feel about the existence and presence of God." One might conclude from a perusal of academic and popular literature that, to use the words of the geographers Julian Holloway and James Kneale, ghosts "can mean many things at once."[23] Yet, specific ghosts haunt for particular reasons, and this is certainly the case with both the ghosts of the present and the demons of spiritual warfare.

Given the pervasiveness of therapeutic discourse, the religious studies scholar Susan Kwilecki suggests that some contemporary communications between ghosts and the living have become part of self-help culture. In studying the 1990s literature on "After-Death Communication," Kwilecki concluded that the movement's "phantoms mirror medical ideals" and suggest to living participants that death "is not, as it might appear, the termination of personal growth—far from it—but rather a new opportunity to expand consciousness and improve relationships."[24] The sociologist Michael Cuneo has linked demons to the same late-modern American therapeutic discourse that Kwilecki harnesses to interpret ghosts. In *American Exorcism*, Cuneo argues that contemporary Catholic, charismatic, and evangelical Protestant exorcism "is remarkably well-suited to the therapeutic ethos of the prevailing culture."[25] In this turn to the explanatory power of the therapeutic, Cuneo and Kwilecki not only register the arguments of scholars such as Illouz, Furedi, and Rieff, but also the theorist Janice Peck's assertions about what she describes as a "psychologized religiosity" shared by celebrities such as Oprah Winfrey, Marianne Williamson, and others. Peck suggests that the self-help, mind-over-matter theologies exhibited by these figures are "isomorphic with a social environment inflected with a modern therapeutic ethos."[26]

These arguments seem persuasive, especially when one considers some late-modern trends. First is the rise of consumer-oriented, identity-peddling, global capitalism that relies on individual desires for uniqueness through commodity purchases. Second is a concomitant focus on individual "projects of the self"; and third is the psychologization and personalization of American public discourse—much of which has the effect of metamorphosing social-structural issues into questions about individuals' moral values and self-worth.[27] In other words, social problems such as stock-market crashes, bank failures, and increasing income equality get personalized as the result of a few bad and immoral people, rather than larger structural and social inequality issues. As the earlier section of this chapter pointed out, there are certainly resemblances between deliverance manuals, self-help literatures, and other cultural goods that promote the healing, transformation, and nurture of the self.

Ghosts—like spiritual warfare's demons—are interstitial beings that exist between the living and dead, the human and the divine. But, even more, they reside in the limbo between the past and the present. The presence of a ghost often suggests some veiled "unfinished business" or "tragedy" in the past that now haunts the present. The social theorist Avery Gordon argues that "haunting and the appearance of specters or ghosts is one way . . . we are notified that what's been concealed is very much alive and present, interfering precisely with those always incomplete forms of containment and repression ceaselessly directed toward us."[28] "Ghosts," the literary scholar Judith Richardson similarly suggests, "operate as a particular, and peculiar, kind of social memory, an alternate form of history-making in which things usually forgotten, discarded, or repressed become foregrounded, whether as items of fear, regret, explanation, or desire." The demons of spiritual warfare serve precisely this function. Their presence notifies those they torment that unfinished business from the past remains and action is required. In what follows, I discuss Third Wave conceptions of how people become haunted and demonized by discussing a selection of deliverance manuals in the hope of illustrating how spiritual warfare's demonic entities—to use Judith Richardson's phrasing—are both "impositions and choices."[29]

CERAMIC CATS AND PORNOGRAPHY

In *Protecting Your Home from Spiritual Darkness*, Glory of Zion International Ministries president Chuck Pierce recounts a purchase he made during a trip to New Orleans. As he walked down the street, something compelled him to stop in front of one particular shop. "In the window," he writes, "was a beautiful ceramic cat with riveting blue eyes." He "seemed drawn to it," and entered the store, which was "filled with oddities, many of which were used in voodoo rituals." Despite this, Pierce's full attention was on the ceramic cat, which he purchased, took home, and placed next to his fireplace. At some point later, Pierce notes, God began revealing to him various "objects in my home that were linked with demonic forces." Walking past his fireplace, he looked at the ceramic cat and "immediately discerned that witchcraft was linked to it." Pierce promptly took the cat statue and ritually destroyed it by passing it through fire and then smashing it.[30]

In explaining how he came to have a demonic ceramic cat in his home, Pierce concluded that his desire for the object was linked to generational inheritances. Specifically, Pierce writes, "I began to see that this cat was linked with spiritism in my bloodline, which is why I was drawn into the voodoo shop in the first place and felt compelled to buy the cat." Pierce suggested that occult activities were present among his ancestors and supported this assertion by recounting how, as a child, he had observed his grandfather using occult powers to kill wasps. "Because I had inherited a weakness toward sins of occult and witchcraft that had been passed down through my family's bloodline," Pierce writes, "that weakness, known as iniquity, was operating in my life when I visited New Orleans and bought the cat."[31]

A second story, told by the deliverance minister and spiritual warfare counselor Ed Murphy, involves a "young, Christian leader" who exhibited "demonic manifestations" during one of Murphy's training sessions. Because Murphy's procedure was "never to deal with serious demonic problems with Christians in public," and since "the man was a strong Christian and the demons fairly easy to control," Murphy waited until the end of the session and then took him to another building to minister to him. Murphy soon encountered "several strong sexual demons" inhabiting the man, "ruling demons" who called themselves "Lust" and "Pornography." After they had revealed themselves to Murphy, he commanded the spirits "to retreat to the stomach of their victim so he had full control of his faculties."[32]

With the demons held temporarily at bay, the counseling session began with Murphy asking the man to tell him "about his sexual activities from his childhood to the present." In the long hours that followed, the man told stories of addiction to pornographic videos and demon-energized intercourse. "So gross was the demonic activity in his life," Murphy noted, "he would sometimes growl like an animal during sexual relations with his wife." "Worst of all," Murphy continued, "he had forced her to watch the videos with him to increase their sexual passions," to the point that "neither she nor her husband could become sexually aroused by one another without the use of the videos." In hearing the man's "sordid story of sexual bondage," Murphy "knew the activity of the evil spirits binding his life would continue until he recognized, confessed, and rejected the sins in his life that had provided the demonic footholds," which Murphy referred to as "sin handles."[33]

Third Wave deliverance manuals are phantasmagoric, yet strictly nonfiction, works that are filled with ghost stories and supernatural events.[34] In story after story, lights turn on and off by themselves, strange odors and mists appear in rooms, feelings of uneasiness envelop people, and apparitions reveal themselves in dark corners and the shadows of the night. But Third Wave theology warns that "ghosts" are really demons and their presence suggests that past sins have become disjunctive forces that infiltrate, dominate, and ruin individual, family, and even community lives. In the two stories above, demons are present because of pasts that haunt. In the first case, the susceptibility to demons has been inherited from the previous generations of a family. Pierce purchases a demon-inhabited ceramic cat because his ancestors' occult proclivities haunt him. He was unwittingly drawn to the object by the unconscious and "iniquitous patterns of sin" passed down through his family's bloodline. In the second story, demons have come to inhabit a man through his own historically habituated pornography use and accompanying lustful thoughts. The man's personal choices, which began in childhood, are now habits that haunt him in his present relationship with his wife. These activities have created "sin handles" to which demons cling. In both cases, the ghosts of the past are the demons of the present.

Evil spirits haunt the Third Wave imaginary and roam the earth. Demons, writes Chuck Pierce, "can inhabit people, objects, portions of land or whole territories, depending on their purpose." They gain access, he continues, "through sin, trauma, victimization, witchcraft, occult practices or cursing."[35] Examining spiritual warfare manuals, one finds several recurring ways in which individuals become demonized, including personal choices and imposed generational curses.

BECOMING DEMONIZED: SINFUL CHOICES

Like the porn-addicted, demon-afflicted pastor, one way people become possessed by demons is through their own sinful choices. Thus, while F. Douglas Pennoyer refers to demonization as a "personal relationship, the imposition of an evil spirit into the life of a human being," such unwelcome impositions are sometimes not "cold calls," but rather are spurred by openings in which the individual—usually unwittingly—has invited a demon into her life by committing sins. Third Wave writers assure readers that Christians can be demonized, and most deliverance rituals are not just performed *by*, but also *on*, spiritual warfare practitioners. While one explanation posited for this is that Satan is invested in directly attacking God's warriors, the Third Wave therapist Ed Murphy suggests another: some Christians were harboring demons prior to their conversion, and the evil spirits remain even after one is born-again. "What I am affirming," writes Murphy, "is that all demons do not automatically leave the body of demonized unbelievers the instant they turn to Christ." Particularly when individuals are severely demonized, Murphy elaborates, and even when they are "brought to Christ through a gospel of power, there is still no guarantee that all of the demons attached to the victim's life will immediately release their hold on the new believer."[36]

The conception of evangelical conversion conjures the image of a dramatic event in which all sins are washed away and the person starts fresh, "born-again" with a new Christian identity that has erased the past.[37] While this view pays heed to the evangelical language of a new birth, it ignores the diversity of views within the movement, including Holiness and Holiness Pentecostal ideas of distinct "second blessings" that occur after conversion and make one free of all voluntary sins.[38] Spiritual warfare deliverance manuals similarly complicate the "born again" concept, suggesting that past demons don't always leave when an individual converts. Sometimes, write the influential 1970s deliverance ministers Frank and Ida Mae Hammond, Christians are so habituated to their demons that "they do not want to change."[39] But, even when they do, full deliverance is not without struggle. Like the addict trying to break the forces of habit that tie him to the source of his addiction, deliverance from demons, Murphy writes, "is more of a process than a once-and-for-all-crisis-event for almost all severely demonized persons."[40]

Murphy suggests that Christians may also become demonized through sinful actions committed after conversion, or through the "serious sin of others committed against him." With regards to the latter, for example, Murphy recounts the story of Jay, a "loud, boisterous, argumentative, and angry" seminary student who wanted to become a pastor, but the faculty considered him a troublemaker. In speaking with Jay, Murphy found that he had been abandoned by his parents at three and was subsequently raised by his physically abusive, alcoholic aunt and uncle. The beatings Jay received, he recounted, pushed him into an incident in which he went outside and screamed his hatred at God, whom he believed had abandoned him. He then called upon Satan to punish his aunt and uncle. Instantly, Jay reported to Murphy, "a dark cloud surrounded me. . . . It still envelopes me," he continued, asking Murphy, "could it be demons?" "I had to go on the assumption that it was," Murphy concluded.[41]

In Jay's story, physical abuse compels a child to make a bad choice. He calls upon Satan for revenge, and this action demonizes him. In other stories, demonization is the result of sinful personal desires, rather than bad decisions brought on by imposed stresses and deprivations. Murphy lists "illicit sexual practices or fantasies" as some of the primary and most potent sins that dominate Christians and incite demonization, and spiritual warfare manuals feature numerous stories of individuals demonized by sexual desire.[42] Eddie and Alice Smith, for example, tell how they delivered a "young pastor's wife" who was being "severely tempted and harassed by demonic spirits." The woman had been involved in "an extramarital affair with a teenage boy who was also a member of their church." After ritually leading her through "repentance, reconciliation, and deliverance concerning the matter," the woman continued to be badgered by evil spirits. Because the Smiths were cognizant that "many Christians have things in their possessions that relate to past sins," they asked the pastor's wife if she had kept any gifts from the boy. She then told them about a necklace and blouse. The Smiths urged the woman to ritually destroy these items, because they were "symbols of the sinful contract she had made with the enemy." The Smiths report that "she and her husband burned the blouse and shattered the necklace, and the attachment was broken, freeing her from her past." In order to banish demons, the Smiths assert, one must remove all the ties that have historically bound the evil spirits to the person: "Remove old love letters; rid yourself of jewelry and clothing that represent and encourage emotional, physical, psychological or spiritual attachment; break free from old things and walk in the newness of God!"[43]

DEMONS IN THE FAMILY: IMPOSITIONS

Demons inhabit a human body when an individual's sinful choices "invite" the evil spirits in.[44] But demons can also take residence without invitation. "Have you ever noticed how," queries Chuck Pierce, "alcoholism, divorce, laziness, or greed tends to run in families?" "These aren't just learned behaviors," he continues, "they are manifestations of iniquity that have been passed down in the generations—in other words—iniquitous patterns."[45] For many scholars, the way to understanding such sorrowful patterns is to examine social conditions and how they reproduce class and family statuses. How and why, they ask, do individuals tend to replicate the same fortunes and fates as their families and peers? This question is a longstanding concern in the social sciences, in particular. Any answer is, of course, complex, inevitably incomplete, and involves—among other things—socialization, enculturation, and unequal material circumstances. In scholarship addressing the problem, the past inequalities of race, class, gender, place, and region haunt the present—often enough to shape it by opening up some possibilities while simultaneously shutting down others. But in deliverance manuals, what is reproduced within the family is not social circumstance but sin. And the underlying causes are not material conditions, but supernatural beings.

In the Third Wave imaginary, demons travel along bloodlines, connecting individuals to their familial pasts through generational curses. While social theorists such as Anthony Giddens and neoliberal economists such as Milton Friedman have proposed a notion of the individual that is increasingly freed from the ascribed identities imposed by family and community, the demonized individual of the Third Wave continues to suffer from the ancestral ties that bind her to sinful forces of habit and their accompanying evil spirits.[46] Murphy suggests that "demons seem to become identified with a family line," and Pierce notes that some of these familial spirits "have been in families for generations on end."[47]

What Third Wave evangelicals see as signs of generational curses, secular people often see as the result of social inequality. Third Wave writers assert that, like those who suffer from material deprivation, individuals who are the victims of a demon in the family experience financial problems, chronic sickness, disease, and premature death. The past replicates itself in the present as "damaged, demonized adults tend to raise damaged, demonized children and grandchildren." But the causes of this are not social and material, but "spiritual." Citing his fellow spiritual warrior, the intercessor Cindy Jacobs, Chuck Pierce lists four activities in which one's ancestors may have engaged that cause generational sin: occult practices and witchcraft, membership in secret societies such as Masons and Shriners, the refusal to tithe ten percent of one's income to God, and the development of sinful habits that become bondages passed on to succeeding generations. In all these cases, an ancestor's "sin is an opening for demonic forces to work in subsequent generations of a family through the iniquity produced."[48]

Third Wave writers claim that theological understandings of Christian scripture must be judged against the reality of experiences with the spirit world. The existence of family demons is no exception. Ed Murphy points out that "direct and clearly defined biblical teachings or examples of demonic transference are not found in Scripture," and thus, biblically speaking, "demonic transference or inheritance would *not* appear likely." Yet, Murphy continues, the "fact" of generational curses and demonic inheritance is proven in practice. He notes that "the experience of most, if not all, believers who are involved in deliverance ministry would reveal this dimension of demonization to be a vivid reality."[49]

This vivid reality is presented in colorful detail. Murphy, for example, recounts his deliverance ministry work with a woman named Betty. "Hers," he writes, "is a story of generational demonization" that "goes back at least five generations, from Betty, through her father, her grandfather, and her great grandfather" and had even "passed on to one of her children." Described as a victim of generational curses and

Satanic ritual abuse—which Murphy asserts "always involves demonic activity"—Betty harbored an unusually large number of demons within her. In his battle to expel the monsters, Murphy discovered that the demonic leader was named "Unbelief," who "turned out to be the prince over all the demons" inhabiting Betty, the total number of which, Murphy confided, was 1,065.[50] In another example, Chuck Pierce relates the story of Cathy, a Christian who suffered from periods of deep depression. Visiting Cathy's house, Pierce was led by God to approach a glass bookcase. "I reached up to the top shelf," Pierce recalls, "and pulled out a copy of the handbook for thirty-second-degree Masons." While Cathy did not know she had the book or even where it had come from, Pierce concluded that her depression was caused by a "Masonic curse in her bloodline." The two built a fire and threw the volume into it in an act of ritual destruction. This book burning began the process of freeing Cathy from her generational inheritance. Eventually, "as the curse was broken," Pierce writes, "the gripping, overwhelming depression that had been Cathy's constant companion completely let go of her mind, and she has walked in freedom ever since."[51]

While Cathy's story had a happy ending, her deliverance from family demons was not immediate. Spiritual warfare manuals resemble secular addiction literature in stressing that getting rid of generational and other evil spirits is a difficult process that takes time and is not always 100 percent successful.[52] Just as becoming demonized is often a gradual process, banishing demons is seldom a one-time event. While Chuck Pierce suggests that "any time we overcome a generational iniquity, it weakens that iniquitous pattern in the blood," he adds the caveat that "sometimes we can do away with it, but sometimes is appears in a weakened form." Rebecca Greenwood tells readers that demons, once banished, always try to regain entrance into a person's life. In Betty's case, Murphy relates that, while she may have had over 1,000 demons expelled, she now battles severe multiple personality disorder and has over 100 alter egos. And Pierce, whose generational curse of occultism led him to purchase the demon-inhabited cat figurine, writes that while he and his wife "have broken many generational iniquities and curses in our own lives," he does "not assume the patterns have been annihilated completely." Because he and his spouse "had difficult childhoods that were mixed with both good and evil inheritances from the generations," they are careful "to always watch our children for signs of recurring patterns of what we know existed in the generations before us." Demons inherited—or brought on by one's own sinful choices—may be forced out, but they can also return. Spiritual warfare manuals include cautionary tales of failed deliverances. These narratives often have tragic endings that include sickness and death, such as the case in which a former Satanist receives deliverance but later returns to his coven and nearly dies from a diabetic coma, or another in which a woman eventually starves to death from a "demon-imposed diet." Murphy warns that "the expulsion of one group of evil spirits from a human life will usually lead to the entry of another group if the sin in the life to which the former demonic spirits had attached themselves is not removed."[53] Forces of habit, like flames, can subside. But they easily flare up again when given sufficient fuel.

EXPELLING DEMONS, REPENTING THE PAST, AND BREAKING FORCES OF HABIT

"I periodically clean out my closet," writes Chuck Pierce. "I find clothes that have emotional ties or inordinate affections with which I associate them." "I may have clothes that do not represent the expression of my personality at the time or outdated garments," he continues, "I also may find clothes that are linked with a season of grief in my life."[54] At first glance, Pierce's detailed description of discarding his old clothes and the logic behind it might seem out of place in a book on banishing demons from your house and possessions (*Protecting Your Home from Spiritual Darkness*). But there is a connection between Pierce's desire to cast off clothes from a previous time in his life and the spiritual warriors' focus on getting rid of demons that haunt because of the past. To paraphrase Eddie and Alice Smith, when demons occupy a person, place, or object, "it will require the ministry of deliverance to evict them."[55] Third Wave practitioners, in delivering the afflicted, are

simultaneously casting out demons and casting off historically inculcated forces of habit. The rituals can be dramatic, but the writers warn
that the results are not always immediate and not always permanent.
The past, it seems, isn't so easy to banish, and demons can return.

Deliverance is the focus of spiritual warfare. It can be performed
on people, places, objects, and even regions or entire countries. An
individual who wants to get rid of demons can sometimes act alone,
but at other times they will need an intercessor to work with them. In
the case of battling principalities and powers (i.e., demons) that control large swaths of land and souls, an intercessory team of a dozen or
more may be needed. But regardless of the level of the battle and the
manpower needed, all deliverance rituals require that the practitioners
prepare themselves. Ed Murphy, for example, provides an appended
"warfare prayer" in his *Handbook of Spiritual Warfare*. The lengthy,
fourteen-paragraph piece begins with the individual reciting that she
bows in worship before God in praise. The spiritual warrior then calls
on the protective power of the blood of Jesus:

> I cover myself with the blood of the Lord Jesus Christ as my protection
> during this time of prayer. I surrender myself completely and unreserv-
> edly in every area of my life to Yourself. I do take a stand against all
> the workings of Satan that would hinder me in this time of prayer, and
> I address myself only to the true and living God and refuse any involve-
> ment of Satan in my prayer.[56]

In *Raising the Devil*, the folklorist Bill Ellis showed that evangelical Protestant—particularly Pentecostal—deliverance ministries have
long utilized "hymns, prayers, and protective charms based on 'The
Blood.'"[57] Sometimes referred to as "pleading the blood," Ellis traces
the ritual appeal to the power of the blood Jesus shed during the cru-
cifixion to an incident recorded in 1907, when a London housewife,
Catherine Jones, utilized it to attain the gift of speaking in tongues.
In spiritual warfare manuals, pleading the blood of Jesus acts both
as a protective armor and a demonic repellent. In other words, the
blood that saves humanity also wards off demons. In the influential,

pre–Third Wave, 1973 deliverance manual *Pigs in the Parlor: The Practical Guide to Deliverance*, Frank Hammond relates what a demon told him about the efficacy of mentioning Jesus' blood. "I commanded the demon to tell me why he could not stand to hear about the blood of Jesus," writes Hammond. "[H]e said, 'because it is so red, because it is so warm, because it is alive, and it covers everything.'"[58]

Murphy's protective battle prayer continues with the warrior reciting praise to God and affirmation of Jesus' victory over evil through his sacrifice and resurrection. The prayer details the spiritual armor that God has given the Christian to fight demons. In addition to donning a "girdle of truth," "breastplate of righteousness," "sandals of peace," and a "helmet of salvation," the practitioner recites, "I lift up the shield of faith against all the fiery darts of the Enemy, and take in my hand the sword of the Spirit, the Word of God, and use your Word against all the forces of evil in my life; and I put on this armor and live and pray in complete dependence upon you, blessed Holy Spirit." The recitation concludes with a final injunction of self-purification that prepares the individual for deliverance work, in which the participant recites that "You have proven your power by resurrecting Jesus Christ from the dead, and I claim in every way your victory over all satanic forces active in my life, and I reject these forces; and I pray in the name of the Lord Jesus Christ with thanksgiving. Amen."[59]

While Hammond's 1973 assertion that everyone needs deliverance is debated in later manuals, the rituals to banish demons all follow a similar structure. First, those performing the deliverance must bind the demon to free the afflicted person's mind. Satan and his demons are bound, while the individual's agency is "loosed." In delivering a son or daughter, for example, the intercessor Cindy Jacobs suggests that one say aloud "Satan, I bind (or tie) you in the name of Jesus!" or "Satan, I bind you and forbid you from operating in my child's life." Murphy asserts that binding not only prevents the demons from interfering with the victim's perceptions of what's going on, but literally quiets the evil spirits during the ritual. He provides a script to this effect, which commands the demons to "be silent until I give you permission to speak."[60]

When Satan and his demons have been effectively bound from action and influence, the afflicted is temporarily freed, or "loosed," from demonic persuasion and must repent of the sins that invited demonization. Chuck Pierce, using a legalistic language common in Third Wave literature (and discussed further in chapter four), explains that "until repentance has occurred and the blood of Jesus is applied, the sin—and thus Satan's legal right to a foothold—remains intact." The second step of deliverance, the act of repentance, makes the "sin handles" that tie the evil spirits to the person disappear—or at least causes them to be more slippery and difficult for the demons to hold on to. Repentance is closely tied to—and often ritually intertwined with—a third stage of deliverance in which the demons are cast out of the individual. Some deliverance ministers command the demons to verbally and physically manifest themselves in the name of Jesus and give their names before leaving the victim's body. In recounting the dramatic deliverance of a child, Ida Mae Hammond tells how she demanded that the demons reveal themselves one-by-one. The six-year-old girl spoke the words of demons, twisted and writhed, and even tore Hammond's blouse. Others performing deliverance sometimes have the victim recite prayers of repentance that simultaneously banish demons. Chuck Pierce, for example, includes a ten-page prayer to be read by individuals demonized by Masonic spirits. Moving through various Freemason "degrees" of membership, the prayers renounce (and thus cast out) specific demonic spirits, including religious figures such as "Brahma," "Allah," and "Anubis," as well as entities such as "The Great Architect of the Universe, who is revealed in this degree as Lucifer, and his false claim to be the universal fatherhood of God."[61]

Earlier deliverance handbooks, such as the Hammonds' *Pigs in the Parlor*, suggested that demons exited via mouths, noses, and even vomit. More recently, the sociologist Michael Cuneo described the practice of vomiting out demons at one North Carolina deliverance church. But contemporary Third Wave deliverance guides are more likely to describe both the afflicted and those who interceded for them as experiencing feelings of "weight" and "darkness" lifting from their bodies and the spaces surrounding them. Third Wave writers assert that there is also occasionally physical evidence that the deliverance was successful. Rebecca Greenwood, for example, relates stories of deliverance in which a person's physical characteristics, such as eye color (God apparently prefers "crystal blue" over "pale green"), change once the demons have been banished.[62] Ideally, if the deliverance is successful, demonic manifestations cease, apparitions and poltergeists disappear, and emotions and attitudes grow more positive.

CONCLUSION

In *The Possession at Loudon*, the French historian and theorist Michel de Certeau writes that "deviltries are at once symptoms and transitional solutions." The focus of his statement was 1630s France—which he described as a traditionally religious society that was "becoming less so"—and an incident involving the demonic possession of nuns. For de Certeau, these demonizations were a highly ritualized enactment of "the confrontation . . . of a society with the certainties it is losing and those it is attempting to acquire."[63] Deliverance guides are the literature of a religious movement that views itself in many ways as at odds with American "secular" culture, and its "deviltries" are both symptoms of and solutions to the Third Wave's ambivalence toward the current cultural moment. Satan's tools for world domination surround them on all sides: other people's religions, multiculturalism, liberal politics, and many forms of popular culture.[64] On the other hand, some of the Third Wave's political and cultural dispositions—the promotion of laissez-faire forms of capitalism as "biblical," theological attacks on what little is left of the welfare state, and the utilization of therapeutic discourse—seem to embrace some of the most dominant themes of the era. The Third Wave both complements and contests some dominant contemporary notions of agency, structure, history, and conceptions of the individual. As will be discussed further in chapter four, the battles with demons described in deliverance manuals register the movement's attraction and repulsion toward the late-modern social formation from which it was born.

Peppered with notions such as generational inheritance and the belief in the propensity for demons to return and torment the afflicted, deliverance manuals suggest a very different conception of self than the notion of an autonomous individual unfettered by her past familial history, social locations, and other historical entanglements. Inheriting your demons from an ancestor or picking them up through a traumatic early childhood experience are undoubtedly examples of impositions, not choices. Yet, in a manner that well expresses the Third Wave's ambivalence toward the notion of a self unfettered by history, stories of deliverance waver between passive victimization and active demonic invitation, between pasts inherited and choices made, between happenstance and willed action. In one example, Eddie Smith recounts the story of Sarah, who as a baby nearly died in an apartment fire. "In her abject fear," Smith writes, "she cried for help, and lingering demonic spirits swept in to 'comfort her.'" This incident is what Third Wave writers such as Rebecca Greenwood call a "root or pillar event," that "original traumatic episode in which spirits of darkness gained entrance." Thus demonized as an infant, the evil spirits inside her compelled Sarah into "making wrong choices and forming alliances with the wrong crowd" as a teenager. "The spirits that had attached themselves to her in her childhood trauma," Smith elaborates, "at this point, because of her sinful choices, were given the opportunity to attract other evil spirits like themselves and thus build a stronghold with which to keep her in bondage." But, readers may wonder, since her "sinful choices" were apparently spurred by the demons already inside her, how much choice did she actually have? Third Wave writers such as Greenwood and Alice Smith tell readers that the victim is always partly to blame for her demon troubles and that "we have to admit that we have the power and prerogative to choose ungodly lifestyles."[65] Yet, stories of trauma such as Sarah's—in addition to tale after tale of innocents inheriting demons from their ancestral bloodlines—suggest a much more conflicted notion of agency.

As will be discussed, Third Wave deliverance manuals reveal much about the inconsistent reverberations of what is sometimes described as contemporary liberal/neoliberal or late-modern conceptions of the self. But the handbooks also register the influence of therapeutic discourse in the way that they mirror self-help manuals. The macro and the micro merge in these works because the ghosts of the past that are the demons of the present are simultaneously *structural* and *individual* "symptoms" and "transitional solutions" within some subjects' life histories. Deliverance practitioners are not simply battling demons, they are simultaneously fighting to expel embodied forces of habit inculcated through haunting pasts. It is in this respect that Third Wave demonology and its practice of deliverance might be dubbed a "Gothic therapeutic."

In his broad study of demon exorcism and deliverance in the United States, *American Exorcism*, Michael Cuneo quips, "personal engineering through demon-expulsion: a bit messy perhaps, but relatively fast and cheap, and morally exculpatory."[66] In spiritual warfare deliverance manuals, narratives about successful demon deliverance certainly abound, but the process usually does not seem as fast and simple—and as cheery—as Cuneo suggests. Spiritual warfare manuals urge the need for a vigilant and continuing offensive, because demons that are expelled often don't stay away. And these deliverances are not morally exculpatory, or at least not entirely. Just because your problems are caused by demons doesn't mean that you are off the hook: you may have brought those demons upon yourself.

In their review of scholarship on the Gothic, Catherine Spooner and Emma McEvoy note that one of its defining elements is an emphasis on a "returning past." This brings to mind Sigmund Freud's "return of the repressed" and, specifically, his concept of "the uncanny," which he described as "nothing new or foreign, but something familiar and old—established in the mind that has been estranged only by the process or repression." Note how deliverance pastor and counselor Ed Murphy dubs deliverance a process and even warns that new demons may replace the old ones banished. Recall that Third Wave writer Chuck Pierce similarly tells readers never to assume that demonically inculcated patterns of behavior are ever completely annihilated, noting that generational demons can be particularly resilient. In his work on the contemporary culture of the Gothic, Mark Edmundsen argues that "addicted" is "our current word for the traditional Gothic term 'haunted.'"[67] While the secular language of addiction is markedly absent in spiritual warfare manuals, the trope of an ongoing, lifelong battle with the haunting ghosts of the past is prominent. As a Gothic therapeutic phenomenon, spiritual warfare's demon expulsions are battles the practitioners hope to win. At the same, however, they realize that a protracted war within and without indefinitely continues.

In his study of Roman Catholic charismatics, the anthropologist Thomas Csordas says that one can learn a great deal about a people from their demons.[68] This is certainly the case with Third Wave demonology. Csordas' study provides a couple of useful comparisons. The demons that fill Third Wave handbooks are—for their authors and probably for most of their readers—real supernatural beings. But they are also forces of habit.[69] Sinful desires indicate the presence of demons. They also signal haunting pasts that have inculcated troublesome patterns of behavior that continue into the present. Recurrent experiences and behaviors develop over time and become habits that are hard to suppress. Sinful activities invite demonic inhabitation, which in turn further encourages more sinful action. In comparing Third Wave with Catholic charismatic deliverance, I agree with Csordas' suggestion that "demonic affliction is uncontrolled habit." I also agree with his assertion that demons named after emotions such as lust or rebellion introduce "an essential ambiguity between internal origin and external cause, between psychological and spiritual, between recognizable human emotions and identifiable demonic influences, between self-possession and demonic possession."[70] I would add to this that such demon names also suggest an ambiguity of agency, with the individual actions of the demonized occurring in the interstice between choice and imposition. But if there is a difference between the Catholic charismatics that Csordas examined and the manuals focused on here, it is that history matters more in Third Wave spiritual warfare.

While Csordas notes that generational curses and the "healing of ancestry" had not found unanimous acceptance among those he studied, the concept is a significant aspect of Third Wave deliverance manuals.[71] Related to the rhetoric of evangelical "new birth" and having sins "washed away," Third Wave writers stress that history matters. The sinful past—conjured by personal choices, generational curses, and traumatic chance occurrences—affects the present and sometimes even controls it. But in expelling demons, spiritual warfare manuals do not seek to completely banish history, but rather to acknowledge and repent for it. One motif of traditional American ghost stories is that the haunting ceases once the tragedies and injustices of the past have been acknowledged and addressed.[72] Similarly, a recurring motif in spiritual warfare deliverance manuals is that, in order to get rid of demons, one must directly confront and repent the sinful past that initially conjured them. Once this "unfinished business" is taken care of, the spirits may depart. But for Third Wave writers—and unlike the most reassuring American ghost stories—they can also reappear. Some historical pasts are so tragic, some forces of habit so ingrained, that demons return and hauntings continue. In this Gothic therapeutic, the past can never be ignored, and is never, ever, erased.

CHAPTER FOUR

HAUNTING DESIRES

AGENCY IN AN ERA OF POSSESSIONS

God gives us all human free will, or the right to make choices.
Rebecca Greenwood, *Breaking the Bonds of Evil*

Bottom line: Who and what your parents and grandparents (and so on) were in their lives directly affects who you become.
Alice Smith, *Beyond the Lie*

"The Lord Jesus is calling you into the bridal chamber of love," writes Alice Smith. "He puts his arms around you and softly whispers, 'come.'"[1] Some intercessors—spiritual warfare's front-line prayer specialists—have taken this statement from Smith to heart, and to bed. Cindy Jacobs relates the story of "Louise" and her sexual relations with a specter she believed to be Jesus. Louise described to Jacobs in detail how she had experienced what she thought was God's intimate method of blessing his mature intercessors. Jacobs writes that "those experiences began when she was awakened in the night and felt every part of her body was charged and alive and a voice told her it was Jesus coming to take her to the bridal chamber." Jacobs was suspicious, because Louise "would become aroused in ways that the Holy Spirit does not do but that were purely demonic." But Louise was convinced, "because the voice was so beautiful and said that it was Jesus, she felt that she must be having some unique experience in which the Lord was loving her in a special way."[2]

Similarly, Rebecca Greenwood describes how she ministered to a group of female intercessors who "were all single and lonely, and greatly enjoyed their friendship with each other and the weekly times of intercession." They shared with Greenwood that they had all been experiencing the same dream in which "Jesus appears and begins to touch them physically and sexually." The women wondered "if this was a gift from the Lord." "Nothing could be further from the truth," Greenwood replied. "Our God would never touch any of His children in a perverse manner" and human relationships with Him are "never sexual."[3] Jacobs came to the same conclusion regarding Louise's case, noting that "we looked for the biblical precedents for intimacy in the Word and saw that those given by God touch us deeply with joy in the spirit, not physical arousal."[4] Rather than Jesus, these intercessors had been tricked into sexual relations with demon lovers. In both cases, the women were "horrified to realize that they had been entertaining demons" and went through rituals of demonic banishment and repentance, asking God to forgive them for "the open invitation to the demonic in their sex lives."[5]

The Third Wave imaginary is haunted by desires. These stories of demon lovers suggest that some longings, especially those of a sexual nature, are particularly problematic because they are satanically inspired. In spiritual warfare manuals, sex certainly plays a prominent role in tales of Christian demonization. But something I find more striking about these stories of intercessors tricked into sex with demons masquerading as Jesus—and just as representative of the movement—is the ambiguity of agency. Clearly, the demons deceived the women in that they disguised themselves as Jesus. Yet, both Jacobs and Greenwood require these women to perform rituals of repentance, with Greenwood going so far as to claim that the lonely, single women offered "open invitations" to demons. Jacobs suggests that Louise allowed the attack because she was unsatisfied in her marriage, in that she believed that "her husband did not give her what she needed in her relationship and that she was bitter toward him for his lack of attention." This "left her an easy mark for the enemy."[6] In other words, they were tricked, but they were also in some way responsible.

In this concluding chapter, I begin by examining—through case studies of sexual desires and human and divine intercession—spiritual warfare conceptions of free will, autonomy, control, and agency. I pick up from the concluding discussions of chapter three and describe how Third Wave theologies of desire and action are complex and seemingly contradictory in their simultaneous insistence upon the powers of individual human choice, demonic compulsion, and the powerful forces of history and family inheritance. On the one hand, these writers continuously deny that the material and social world can push and propel people into sinful actions by stressing the conscious and willful nature of human sin. On the other hand, these same authors appear to suggest that both biological drives and demon spirits thrust individuals into sinful activities, and humans do not always have full control over their consciousness and faculties. This vacillation between autonomous free-will individualism and external compulsion is not particular to Third Wave evangelicals, but is a typical and persistent theme across vast swaths of the contemporary American landscape.

After suggesting this, I segway into the second half of the chapter, a book-concluding examination of the shared and exclusive elements between spiritual warfare and the contemporary social imaginary known as "neoliberalism." I describe how—in addition to touting the reality of a free, autonomous human self—the Third Wave theology of biblical economics, its legalistic language of property and individual rights, and belief of the force of spirit over matter all mirror neoliberal ideas. Yet, at the same time, spiritual warfare's demonologies suggest that the forces of history, materiality, and the social world continue to ghost the present and propel individuals into activities and lives that are not of their own choosing. In effect, spiritual warfare's demons represent a return of the repressed, in that the forces ignored and denied in the neoliberal imaginary reappear, demanding recognition that they continue to possess the late-modern human agent.

DEMON LOVERS

To defeat and escape the snare of the world system, we must identify its lies, die to its appeal, and focus our attention and affection upon our gracious God. To defeat the desires of the flesh, we must refuse to acknowledge or accommodate it. More than that, we must literally run away from lustful temptations. Bottom line: We must stop giving our flesh what it wants by no longer yielding to its demands.

Eddie Smith, *Breaking the Enemy's Grip*

According to spiritual warfare handbooks, it is the desires of the flesh—mentioned by Eddie Smith in the preceding quote—that seem most likely to snare Third Wave evangelicals. According to Third Wave counselor Ed Murphy, "demons of sexual abuse and perversion are floating in the air" and are "among the most active, subtle, and vicious of all demons." This is quite a statement, considering that there are demons of murder, apostasy, and the occult also fluttering about in the ether. Murphy mirrors other writers when he suggests that "illicit sexual practices and out of control fantasies" constitute the first of four "primary sin areas" in which demon-harassed Christians battle. In the Third Wave imaginary, demons and the biology of sexual desire combine to make such a powerful stimulant that even intercessors themselves should never work alone with demon-fighters of the opposite sex, since "more often than not, an affair will be the outcome" because "the enemy will use the opportunity to create an open door of physical attraction between the two parties."[7]

Cindy Jacobs warns readers that "Satan will send demons of lust, perversion or fantasy to try to open a door for him to send along a temptation to get you to fall into sin." Jacobs elaborates that the Devil sends sexual dreams, visitations by incubi or succubae (male and female sexual demons), and other humans into Christians' lives to lead them into sexual sin. For God's soldiers, the torment is constant, and deliverance from sexual demons—like all demons—does not guarantee they are gone forever. Rebecca Greenwood shares the story of Tina, a Christian who was plagued with the "spirit of perversion," delivered from it through intercessory prayer, but then again tempted. Tina "succumbs to the advances of a demon" when her husband is out of town. In addition to taking on the persona of Jesus, as seen in the story that opened this chapter, demons will even disguise themselves as deceased spouses and lovers. Cindy Jacobs relates the example of Gloria, whose deceased fiancé began visiting her at night for sex. A suspicious intercessor friend of Gloria's prayed to God to show her friend who the spirit really was. The prayer was successful, and the spirit's true demonic nature was revealed when, one night, Gloria "saw him lying on her couch, but to her utter shock his form was disgusting and revolting."[8]

Spiritual warfare writers warn that intimacy, even when it is initially nonsexual, is problematic—and potentially demonic. Jacobs notes that intimate nonsexual relationships between prayer partners of the opposite sex can lead to "strong ties of affection" that result in "spiritual adultery," while Greenwood cautions that sexual relationships and even close friendships can lead to demons being passed from one person to another. "Soul ties," Greenwood writes, "are emotional and spiritual connections between those who jointly engage in sinful practices." Greenwood asserts that "all forms of sexual sin" and intense childhood friendships can establish soul ties that allow the demonic to "transfer" between people. In the stories found in spiritual warfare manuals, the demons garnered from soul ties are particularly pernicious when the person who passes on the evil spirits is involved in occult activities such as voodoo and satanism. And one's long-ago high school sexual relationships—even without the occultism—can cause a plague of lustful spirits. Greenwood relays the tale of one married woman who, many years before, had sex with her high-school boyfriend. The woman was inundated with sexual dreams and needed intercessory prayer to help break "the power of the ungodly tie of perversion, whoredom, and lust operating between the two of them."[9] Following the prayer, the woman remembered that she had saved all the love letters and cards from her high-school beau in the attic. She destroyed them all, and that act, along with the prayer, freed her from the tormenting sexual demons.

But Satan and his minions are not all we have to contend with. Even without the constant assaults by demons of lust and perversion who foment the establishment of sinful soul ties, spiritual warfare writers assert that the human sex drive is so strong, in itself, that it will often lead Christians to sin. Ed Murphy tells of one young female missionary who was seduced by an older female missionary. Murphy asserts that the younger woman "knew it was wrong, but once she was sexually stimulated there was no turning back." In another narrative, Murphy divulges how one male "Christian leader" fought back the nearly uncontrollable urge to have sex with and even rape someone immediately after seeing a burlesque show.[10]

In Third Wave manuals, sexual urges appear almost uncontrollable and sexual identity and preferences seem fragile and easily changed. As with Murphy's story of the missionaries, heterosexual Christians who are subject to strong biological urges or are damaged by past traumatic events can quickly become involved in bisexual and homosexual relationships. In one example, Rebecca Greenwood asserts that a woman who, as a child, suffered physical and mental abuse at the hands of her father, became a lesbian because of it. In another, Freudian-style tale, Greenwood relates how one woman became a chronic masturbator with bisexual desires because she saw her parents walk around the house nude when she was growing up.[11]

Despite these demonic and biological compulsions, Third Wave authors continue to stress human choice. In discussing a married Christian pastor who had multiple affairs, Murphy concludes that "even if a strong demonic dimension to his sexual licentiousness existed, the pastor was still responsible for his actions. . . . To sin or not is a choice."[12] And, as noted above, Jacobs, Greenwood, and others consistently require that those tricked into trysts with demons repent for believing the lies they had been told by the spirits they thought to be Jesus or a deceased fiancé. But the language about the boundaries between free will and compulsion is slippery. In Murphy's story, a sexually stimulated missionary is physically unable to stop a homosexual encounter, even though she knows it is wrong, because her biological drive has taken over. Yet, in another tale by the same author, the adulterous pastor is still at fault even if he is under demonic control. In spiritual warfare parlance, "doors have been opened" and "invitations" to the demonic delivered, even when the human is not fully cognizant of doing it. This ambiguity of agency goes beyond the morass of human sexual desire to include the relationship between God and his Third Wave generals, the intercessors.

INTERCESSION

In Third Wave circles, intercessors are the agents God uses to "enforce his will" on earth. They are called by God to act on his behalf to battle Satan and his demonic minions directly. Cindy Jacobs, for example, writes that "God spoke to me one day and said, 'Cindy, I want you to lay your ministry down and learn to intercede.'" Intercessors can be male or female, adult or child. They are expected to fast, meditate, and pray, to purify their hearts and then wait for a message from God that tells them what to do. When they receive the message, this "gift of intercession" manifests itself through physical sensations, emotions, dreams, and thoughts that God sends to guide the spiritual warrior toward people in need of help. Rebecca Greenwood notes that God sends her physical clues that reveal information about demonic activities. She writes that "sometimes I feel heat on my ears and hands, signaling an anointing for deliverance and healing." Greenwood adds that she feels cold when the spirit of death is near, and "when I am in the presence of witchcraft, I experience spinning or dizziness around my head, and many times it feels as if the ground is moving under my feet."[13]

Spiritual warfare authors suggest that intercession plays a prominent role in history. Cindy Jacobs touts the immense supernatural power of multiple intercessors praying about the same thing and asserts that "every time history is made moving circumstances toward the will of God, intercessors have been there first." Harold Caballeros concurs, writing that he is a "completely convinced witness that intercessory prayer is the way to change history." Third Wave founder and figurehead Peter Wagner even suggests that contemporary intercessors have the same powers that Jesus demonstrated during his lifetime. He writes that "my theological premise is the following: The Holy Spirit was the source of all of Jesus' power during his earthly ministry." "Jesus exercised no power of or by Himself," Wagner continues.

"[W]e today can expect to do the same or greater things than Jesus did because we have been given access to the same power source."[14]

Given the extremely powerful effect intercessors and their prayers are thought to have, it is not surprising that spiritual warfare handbooks are filled with miracle stories. Harold Caballeros asserts that intercessory prayer and fasting in his country of Guatemala led to the election of the nation's first "Christian" (read evangelical) president. In *Possessing the Gates of the Enemy: A Training Manual for Militant Intercession*, Cindy Jacobs claims that intercessory prayers made Nazis retreat in a World War II battle and, in the late 1980s, led to the dismantling of the Berlin Wall. She suggests that her own intercessory prayers, performed while aboard a plane, actually lessened the harmful effects of an American stock-market crash. In addition to these dramatic events, Jacobs asserts that the intercessory prayers she and other colleagues engaged in kept an alcohol-free town dry, halted the construction of a Muslim school, swayed a court case in favor of school Bible clubs, converted a San Francisco Wiccan high priest, and saved a missionary from being murdered by a mob of Muslims on the other side of the globe in Indonesia.[15]

In addition to the more public and bigoted political outcomes cited by Jacobs earlier, intercessory prayers also result in personal miracles. As seen in chapter three, more often than not, intercessory prayer is used to help drive demons away from tormented individuals who seek to be freed from affliction. But such prayers can also work to heal physiological and emotional problems. Rebecca Greenwood, for example, asserts that intercessory prayer made one boy's autism symptoms partially subside and even provided a lonely young girl with a "special best friend" at her school.[16] Third Wave stories suggest that there is nothing too large or too insignificant to be changed by the power of prayer. And like spiritual warfare tales about sex, intercessor narratives reveal complex conceptions of agency.

First, the language used suggests that God is as dependent on intercessors to do work on earth as intercessors are dependent upon God to gift them with intercessory powers and directions. Note how the phrasing implies mutual need in the relationship and a shared agency when Cindy Jacobs writes that "He nudges you to pray so that He can intervene." "God," she continues, "will direct you to pray to bring forth His will on earth as it is in heaven." God is all-powerful in Third Wave theology, an entity that could seemingly alter history without human help. Yet, one gets the idea that the God imagined in spiritual warfare has set up the game so that the rules require humans to actively work on his behalf. Ed Murphy tells readers that curses "worked up" by satanic magic can only be overcome by "the greater power of God," but that, sometimes, God "does not automatically overcome these curses on our behalf," because he wants us "to learn the world of spirit curses and break them ourselves" through "group spiritual warfare praying."[17]

Second, the miracle stories suggest—without explicitly saying—that intercessors can, with God's help, change the motivations and activities of other humans through prayer. Prayers can bring a lonely girl a friend, cause a judge to rule in favor of conservative Christian policies, and stop people from selling off stocks and thus decrease the damage of a stock-market crash. In all of these examples, individuals are moved to act differently because powerful prayers they are not conscious of somehow sway them. Such prayers appear like the "world images" created by ideas in Max Weber's social theory that "have, like switchmen, determined the tracks along which action has been pushed."[18] Given the power of intercession, how much agency is granted in this to the friend who appeared, the judge who ruled, and the people who held on to their stocks?

As we have seen, the question of agency with regard to those who are demonized through generational inheritance or stumble into encounters with demon-riddled objects and places can be perplexing. While Third Wave evangelicals rhetorically assert and reassert free will and choice, the stories they tell include traumatized infants succored by demons disguised as imaginary friends, innocents inheriting evil spirits that run in their family because of great-grandfathers, and families demonized in their houses because of sins committed on the land by strangers in the long-distant past. Agency swerves and swirls in the Third Wave imaginary, as humans are "freely compelled" to engage in actions.

FREELY COMPELLED

Spiritual warfare handbooks generally discuss agency in one of three ways, ranging from phrasings that suggest humans have little choice, to those that affirm complete autonomy and free will. At times, humans seem to be pushed and propelled by familial forces over which they have little control. Alice Smith tells readers that a "generational stronghold is an influence, open door, or trait that causes us to think, believe, and behave in a manner contrary to God's truth," something that "provokes and perpetuates repeated behaviors from generation to generation."[19] At other times, the force that compels is not demonic and familial, but satanic and structural. Harold Caballeros writes that Satan uses structures, including ideologies, culture, and idiosyncrasies, "to enslave men."[20] These structures create "ways of thinking that are contrary to the Word of God, to separate men from the divine plan, and in doing so, reduces them to slavery."[21] Similarly, spiritual mapping founder George Otis tells readers that the "course of history" and its "confluent events will play a major role in defining the life and character of a community."[22] Because of this, Otis argues, the alcoholism he observes in the Canadian indigenous communities that he studies are not just the result of contemporary social injustices, but also "the legacy of ancient spiritual pacts" the First Nation peoples made with evil spirits.[23] This explanation resembles the televangelist and occasional presidential candidate Pat Robertson's 2010 comment that the Haitian earthquake was caused by a pact the country's founders made with Satan.[24] Robertson received a deluge of negative press after claiming that, in 1804, Haitian slaves made a contract with Satan to be freed from French slavery and had thus cursed the country for future generations. But few if any members of the media seemed cognizant of the fact that this was not Robertson's quirky personal belief, but rather an idea taken from Third Wave theology. What is striking here about both Otis' and Robertson's arguments, though, is that contemporary Canadian Indians and present-day Haitians, through no apparent fault of their own, are suffering tragedies and deaths because of curses brought on by ancestors who lived hundreds of years ago. Free will and choice seem irrelevant when it comes to these contemporary victims.

But, in other cases, Third Wave authors suggest that agency is found somewhere between the human and the demonic forces hounding her. For Third Wave evangelicals, Christians cannot be "possessed" by demons, because they see that term suggesting full demonic control over the human, which conflicts with the theology of free will. Instead, spiritual warfare manuals will use words such as "influenced," "oppressed," and "demonized" to suggest the gradations of demonic power over the individual. As noted earlier, this clinging to choice and free will makes explaining certain forms of demonic torment difficult. In one passage, for example, Ed Murphy writes that most individuals don't choose to come under demonic influences and notes that this is especially the case when people have been "demonized from infancy or childhood." But he continues by asserting that "God still holds them responsible for their choices" because humans, though fallen, "still bear the image of God." He writes that "we possess the right and the capability to resist the entrance of demons into our lives if we are aware of what is occurring."[25]

"If we are aware of what is occurring." That last line would seem to be a major "if," but Third Wave writers strive to suggest that even in the most convoluted cases in which demons sneak into individuals' lives, the person must always have had some choice in the matter. In describing what she calls "the closest case I have witnessed to one of demonic possession," Rebecca Greenwood tells the story of Hannah, a suicidal woman who had been "raised in a home of Satan worshipers." Even in this case, Greenwood says she is "cautious" about referring to the case as possession, because "controlling ownership cannot be taken; it can only be given over by the victim." For his part, Murphy ultimately concludes that "regardless of how demons are able to gain entrance into human lives either in infancy or in later adulthood, the Bible always holds the individuals accountable for their actions." This is because, "regardless of the amount of control demons presently exercise their victims at one point had enough authority to resist their evil desires."[26]

These writers seem to be struggling to define the nature and limits of human agency in some types of demonic oppression, even though they consistently affirm free will. Indeed, statements about human autonomy are common throughout spiritual warfare manuals. Rebecca Greenwood tells readers that "God gives all humans free will, or the right to make choices," while Alice Smith asserts that "humans aren't puppets—we have moral freedom for which we, not God, are responsible." "He created us not as robots but as moral agents with the ability to make decisions," Smith reiterates.[27] We are not puppets or automatons, but moral agents with free will and the ability to make decisions. These are the affirmations spiritual warfare authors make. And yet, contrary to this, the stories of demonic generational inheritance and satanic structures, Haitian earthquakes and inherited alcoholism, all suggest that humans cannot—even in the Third Wave imaginary—willfully divorce themselves from history and the social/familial world in which they exist. I don't point this out to "catch" these demon-busting evangelicals at being inconsistent. Of course they are, but as more than enough scholars, songwriters, and poets have pointed out, the mesh of ideas, concepts, and activities that human beings engage with are seldom coherent.[28] Quite the contrary, I suggest that the Third Wave affirmation of human agency and free will, even in the face of its own narratives of generational inheritance and compelling satanic structures, is a common tactic across multiple contemporary social worlds.

One recurring—though largely unmarked—way that American religious movements have historically understood and explained social inequalities could be described as "economic arminianism," which developed within nineteenth-century evangelical revivalism.[29] In this theology, the individual holds full responsibility for both her heavenly and earthly fates. One's poverty or wealth, like one's damnation or salvation, are entirely matters of individual free will. In other words, economic arminianism asserts that poverty always results from individual shortcomings, if not plain sinfulness. Conversely, wealth is fully the result of one's will and is often also a sign of God's favor. Stretching from nineteenth-century writers such as Henry Ward Beecher to contemporary prosperity gospel ministers such as Creflo Dollar, New Age mediums, the Ayn Rand–inspired plans of 2012 vice presidential candidate Paul Ryan, the biblical economics of Third Wave evangelicals such as Cindy Jacobs, and certain segments of the Tea Party, economic arminianism has been one of the most prominent and malleable social and religious doctrines in American religious history.

Living in a period that some have called the new Gilded Age, Americans today face the greatest economic disparities between the rich and poor since such things began to be reliably recorded. Hearing that your social class is completely the result of your own smarts, your own choices, your ability to think positively, and even your moral state—such things spiritually congratulate the elite and comfortable. And such notions may even provide those less fortunate with some hope that they can change things through pure will. At the very least, these assertions hearten the self-described biblical capitalists in Wisconsin, seen in 2011 holding signs declaring that "God Hates Taxes" and claiming that unions and the minimum wage were satanic. From the early nineteenth century to the present, economic arminianism has provided a supernatural explanation of social difference. This theology, dependent upon the existence of autonomous, free-willed individuals, has offered a divine apologetics for class inequalities. In blessing the rich, the poor get damned. The socioeconomic forces and material conditions that lay outside any one person's control disappear, replaced by conjurations of individual will, free choice, and moral status.

Note, at this point, how much these manifestations of economic arminianism complement certain contemporary notions of agency, structure, history, and conceptions of the individual—specifically these ideas as they are conceived within the conglomeration of economic, political, and cultural activities and ideologies known as "neoliberalism." Third Wave evangelicalism was born in a neoliberal era, and it reverberates with the characteristics and inconsistencies of the neoliberal imaginary.

THE LATE-MODERN NEOLIBERAL IMAGINARY

"Neoliberalism" is a term shunned by some historians, embraced by many social theorists, and often ill-defined by people across the academic spectrum. It is used much more often than it is defined. Given this, some elaborations are due. Though there were historical precedents, in the United States, neoliberalism first came to prominence in association with Milton Friedman and the University of Chicago's School of Economics in the 1960s.[30] Politically, it was promoted by Ronald Reagan and Margaret Thatcher in the 1980s and Bill Clinton in the 1990s. In the twenty-first century, its span is global and it influences nearly all aspects of everyday life. The social theorist Pierre Bourdieu suggests that this "free trade faith" is "not just one discourse among many," but rather one that seems all-encompassing, inevitable, and natural because "it has on its side all of the forces of a world of relations of forces, a world that it contributes to making what it is."[31]

Neoliberalism is foremost a laissez-faire capitalist economic philosophy that envisions worldwide free markets unfettered by government restrictions and national boundaries. Proponents of neoliberalism often argue against regulations by using legalistic language about individual property and human rights (both crucial elements for functioning free markets). "Deregulation" and "choice" are its key terms. The neoliberal economic model plays down the notion of the "social" and imagines atomistic, autonomous, and rational individuals who have the complete free will to participate in consumer capitalist markets, which are envisioned as independent from all other spheres of life. At its most extreme, and exemplified by Margaret Thatcher's 1987 comment, society simply ceases to exist. "There is no such thing as society," Thatcher declared, "There are individual men and women and there are families."[32] The historian Bethany Moreton writes,

> Thus neoliberalism envisions the economy as a sphere independent of other social institutions and relationships. It understands the market to operate by natural laws that will, if left to their own devices, optimize the conditions of human existence. In this logic, there is no such thing as society or community, only individuals; the commons are a crime against efficiency; and government action intrudes illegitimately on the sovereign territory of economics, to the detriment of all.[33]

Neoliberalism denies society's power to shape human subjectivities, instead imagining a free-willed, autonomous individual unaffected by material circumstance. It also decontextualizes and dehistoricizes human agents and their objects, in effect de-culturing the world in a way that allows commodities (and, according to Olivier Roy, religions) to be sold and consumed transnationally by diverse individuals in sundry places.[34] At its core, then, it depends upon a fancifully imagined human subject that is completely unfettered by its history and social locations. Neoliberalism, write the anthropologists Jean and John Comaroff, "re-visions persons not as producers from a particular community, but as consumers in a planetary marketplace: persons as ensembles of identity that owe less to history or society than to organically conceived qualities."[35]

In his intellectual history of the United States in the late twentieth and early twenty-first centuries, *Age of Fracture*, the historian Daniel Rodgers argues that the stress on the individual and the declining acknowledgement of the power of the social was a trend that permeated multiple cultural fields. Rodgers argues that, from the late 2000s to the present,

> One heard less and less about society, history, and power and more about individuals, contingency, and choice. The importance of economic institutions gave way to notions of flexible and instantly acting markets. History was said to accelerate into a multitude of almost instantaneously accessible possibilities. Identities became fluid and elective. Power thinned out and receded.

But it wasn't that social forces actually ceased to influence and habituate. Rather, Rodgers suggests, "in an age of Oprah, MTV, and charismatic religious preaching, the agencies of socialization were different from before, but they were not discernibly weaker." "What changed," he continues, "across a multitude of fronts, were the ideas and metaphors capable of holding in focus the aggregate aspects of human life as opposed to its smaller, fluid, individual ones."[36] While he does not use the term, Rodgers' description here well describes what I see as the linguistic effects of what I will call the late-modern neoliberal imaginary. By this phrase, I mean that lexicon of terms, practical programs, embodied habits, and performed activities that desocializes, decontextualizes, dehistoricizes, and—ultimately—*dematerializes* the world.

Though the words one has to choose from make it difficult, my intention in this discussion is to avoid an overly simplistic, ahistorical and structuralist argument. It would be easy to envision the various ideas that fall under the term "neoliberalism" into a newly constituted scenario that singly controls and propels the Third Wave and other religious practices and ideas. The first pitfall to avoid is that of ahistoricity. I realize that conceptions of autonomous individuals, free-market choice, and processes of desocialization and dehistoricization existed in "liberalism" long before the word "neoliberalism" was ever spoken. At the same time, it would be naïve to assert that contemporary, late-modern alterations in work-life, welfare programs, shifts from industrial to consumer capitalism, transnational trade, mass-media globalization and homogenization, and concomitant changes in sources of self-identity have no effect on or relationship to religious imaginaries. In other words, there is no doubt that there are historical precedents to the characteristics I am grouping under the term "neoliberalism." But the combining of these things in the contemporary period—a modernity described with modifiers such as "accelerated," "late," "liquid," and "extreme"—entails something new and different.

The other pitfall to avoid in engaging in a serious discussion about neoliberalism and its ties to religion is that of structuralism. A vital question in both the humanities and social sciences regards the extent to which we have the ability to think and act freely in a social world that seemingly works at every moment to constrain what we are capable of conceiving and doing.[37] The relationship between the actions of individuals and groups and the larger social structures within which they reside is complex, and to presume autonomous individuals making free choices in a religious marketplace is just as problematic as imagining a structural determinism that takes the occasional unpredictable anomalies of human action totally out of the picture. While the latter denies the multiple and often conflicting activities that tend to perpetuate structures, the former engages in the neoliberal fantasy that material realities and social groupings are mere phantoms.[38] Neoliberalism certainly has produced structures that compel particular historical and material consequences. The neoliberal imaginary also blends ideas about human subjects, social models, and economic theories in ways that make certain conceptions of the world and its inhabitants seem more legitimate and "natural" than others.

In thinking about ways to describe how certain late-modern neoliberal institutions, ideas, and materializations are registered in Third Wave spiritual warfare, I landed upon a term relating to sound: "reverberation."[39] Reverberation is the continuation of a musical note or sound that persists after the act that made the initial tone has ended. Imagine an electric bass guitarist and drummer together in a small, echoey room. In the song they are about to play, the bass guides the piece's structure. Also, the bass guitarist has tuned her strings to lower octaves, which not only makes the notes rumble, but—when run through her loud, high-wattage tube amplifier—assures that a single-string pluck creates a long sustaining hum that thunderously reverberates throughout the band practice space.[40] It vibrates the metal rattles on the bottom of the snare drum, which then registers the bass hum by making its own sound (even though the drummer did not hit the snare). The drum is independent of the bass guitar. It makes its own sounds when the drummer strikes it with her stick. But the drums follow the bass's lead in the song. In addition, the force of the bass guitar sustain in this case is so powerful that its activities bleed into the snare, shaping and adding to the drum's sound even when it is being played. I suggest that the structures of late-modern neoliberalism—like the bass guitar—thunderously reverberate throughout the Third Wave movement, shaping the movement's cadence to greater or lesser effect in different contexts.

FIGHTING DEMONS IN THE NEOLIBERAL ERA

The loose-knit conglomeration of Protestants that make up the Third Wave clearly embrace neoliberal ideas of human free will, individualism, globalization, free-market capitalism, and the political and commercial agents and structures that promote such things. Bethany Moreton has argued that there is a soul to neolberalism, and I am not alone in suggesting that the Third Wave and its theological relatives house it.[41] As noted by scholars such as Birgit Meyer, Kevin Lewis O'Neill, and David Martin, missionizing by neo-Pentecostals (the group that, along with Protestant charismatics, make up the bulk of Third Wave participants) has frequently gone hand-in-hand with the development of neoliberal forms of capitalism around the world, especially in Africa and Latin America.[42] Meyer argues that "Pentecostal Christianity has become enmeshed with the neo-liberal environment into which it seeks to spread. . . . PCCs embrace and seek to transform the 'world,' seizing the consumerist possibilities and media technologies offered by neo-liberal capitalism."[43] Given this, it should not be surprising that Third Wave ideas about economics, their language about legal rights, and promotion of spirit over matter—in addition to their conception of humans as autonomous and freely willed—closely resemble neoliberal conceptions.

In terms of economy, spiritual warfare authors and fellow travelers such as Edward Silvoso suggest that God prefers capitalism, and prayer can bring prosperity.[44] Writers such as Alice Patterson and Cindy Jacobs are representative of Third Wave leaders in suggesting that God specifically prefers a "biblical economics" of laissez-faire systems with no regulation and no social safety nets. "Have you ever entertained the thought," writes Patterson, "that the Bible speaks to almost every circumstance in life—including fiscal governmental issues?"[45] Likening God to an industrial capitalist, Jacobs refers to the Bible as "the Manufacturer's handbook" and says it is where we must look to "see what the Creator instituted in His economic structure."[46] In Patterson's reading, the Bible reveals that God never took away from the rich to give to the poor, never required the rich to tithe more, and includes stories suggesting that a minimum wage "is against the word of God" and caring for young widows and single mothers is "certainly not the responsibility of the government."[47] In the Third Wave imaginary, poverty is often seen as a curse for breaking God's law.[48] When

Cindy Jacobs writes that she had made a mistake praying for a woman to receive financial help because "her financial need had resulted from disobedience" and had thus unwittingly "prayed against the dealings of God in her life," she perfectly conjures the dispositions of economic arminianism.[49] Her words are nearly interchangeable not only with other contemporary Christian Right and Tea Party favorites such as David Barton and Paul Ryan, but also with those of Russell Conwell, who, in his Gilded Age *Acres of Diamonds* sermon, asserted that "to sympathize with a man whom God has punished for his sins, thus to help him when God would still continue a just punishment, is to do wrong, no doubt about it, and we do that more than we help those who are deserving."[50]

But Jacobs and some other Third Wave authors go much further than Conwell in elaborating an economic theology. "Reversing the Genesis Curse," the name of a chapter in her 2008 *Reformation Manifesto*, borrows from the conservative Christian economist Tom Rose to assert that "biblical economics" is strongly supply-side and free-market-oriented.[51] Because of Adam and Eve's sin, Jacobs explains, the land was cursed with scarcity, but when Jesus "came to reverse the fall, He not only paid the price for our sin, but according to Galatians 3:13-14, broke the curse and its effects: scarcity, want, and lack." This atoning "removal from the curse of the law" is read by Jacobs to suggest that any economic model based on limited resources and scarcity is unbiblical. This is the primary problem with Keynesian economics, which Jacobs describes as an atheistic "mindset that we live in a finite world," and "if we are all a cosmic accident, we must control what little we have, as there is no way to get more." She goes on to blame this economic model of scarcity for abortion and birth control, ultimately suggesting that "we must view the world through the lens of an unlimited God, not temporary limitations to our supply of resources."[52]

In other words, to believe that natural resources such as oil are finite and nonrenewable is false materialist thinking. Because God is an infinite being, any model of economics must be one of infinite abundance. New schools of economics, particularly "supply-side and free market economics," Jacobs writes (without using the term "neoliberal"), "basically function from a prosperity mentality and are much more biblical in their worldview" because they say to "just leave people alone and they will naturally do what is in their own self-interest to grow the economy, just as water flows downhill." In such a laissez-faire system, "prosperity will then affect all who are willing to work for it." This phrasing of the fantastical fantasy of the unfettered market could have come from a speech by any of neoliberalism's saints: Ayn Rand, Milton Friedman, Margaret Thatcher, or Ronald Reagan. But Jacobs adds an explicitly supernatural element (though no more magical) that earlier neoliberal proponents generally eschewed. Jacobs asserts that, "it is entirely possible for God to give his children a plan to eradicate systemic poverty," though, she adds, "it can only be done supernaturally." "It is possible," she continues, "to see the kingdom of God so manifested in a nation that there is no need for a welfare system at all—especially for any believer!"[53]

In addition to the promotion of neoliberal economic models as biblical, Third Wave evangelicals discuss human bodies and property using a language of legal rights that mirrors contemporary neoliberal discourses on human rights, in which such rights are tied to property and the liberty to consume and own.[54] The supernatural world, both good and evil, works through contracts and rights. "All Christians carry authority over demons," writes Rebecca Greenwood, "because we are members of the army of God, we have the legal right to exert power over the enemy in the name of Jesus." At the same time, Alice Smith warns readers that Jesus' sacrifice on the cross does not nullify "pacts we've made with powers of darkness." She writes that "we are still responsible to cancel any contracts" we have made with the demonic and that, "until we do, the enemy has the legal right to enforce the agreement." "Demons know their legal rights," Greenwood elaborates, "if the victim opens the door for them by sinning, they will make full use of their authority to inflict harm." Intentional, habitual, and generationally inherited sins, Eddie Smith explains, "can become a legally binding spiritual contract (or agreement) that one knowingly or unknowingly makes with the enemy." And this language is repeated, as seen in chapter two, with respect to one's property. Greenwood tells readers that "landowners have legal authority to confront demonic activity on their land," "territorial rights" to that which we own.[55] Third Wave evangelicals imagine that the supernatural world of demons—like the Chinese spirit realm—is subject to the same legal rules as the material world. Indeed, the legal obligations we incur in the spiritual world are much more important than those of our everyday lives. "In truth," Rebecca Greenwood writes, "the spiritual realm of good and evil is more real and alive than the physical realm in which we live."[56]

This valuation of spirit over matter blends with the promotion of a "biblical economics" of unlimited resources and the concept of free-willed autonomous individuals to produce a discourse that tends to deny the power of the social, material world. But, as seen in the chapters of this book, the Third Wave movement has a much more ambivalent relationship to these concepts than it might initially seem. While history, materiality, and the social might rhetorically be deemed insignificant, the demons that spiritual warfare practitioners battle so fiercely seem to represent these very things. And demons, it seems, are not going away any time soon.

CONCLUSION

Demons—at least in the media and in polling—have increased their visibility since I first started working on this subject in 2010. In a May 2014 *Washington Post* article, one can read about how the otherwise modern Pope Francis is "old school" when it comes to Satan and his demonic minions, who have apparently ramped up their attacks enough that there is increasing demand for priests to perform exorcisms. The *New York Times Book Review* recently featured *Demon Camp*, the journalist Jennifer Percy's study of an Iraqi War vet who practices deliverance ministry to help other veterans, while The Oprah Network's *Our America with Lisa Ling* premiered its third season with an episode, "Fighting Satan," on deliverance ministries. One poll from fall 2013 suggests that 51 percent of Americans think that an individual can be "possessed by the devil or some other evil spirit." Demons seem to be everywhere, and the Third Wave and its demon-infested theology of spirit over matter is more commonplace than academics have imagined.[1]

Writing about African Pentecostals, Jean Comaroff notes that "in their personal circumstances, metaphysical forces seem more palpable in the pattern of unfolding events than do intangible forces such as society, economy, and history."[2] The privileging of the spirit world over the material one is a prominent theological point in spiritual warfare handbooks. George Otis Jr. complains that those who have "embraced the language and worldview of the Enlightenment" dismiss spiritual explanations. "Ask them to explain why things are the way they are in communities," he asserts, "and they will instinctively turn to the oracles of sociology, economics, or politics."[3] Third Wave practices such as spiritual mapping, therefore, are ways of seeing "the world around us as it really is, not as it appears to be," in Peter Wagner's words.[4] This statement could well sum up the general goal of many classical theorists who initiated or utilized a hermeneutics of suspicion. For a Marxist, one objective is to lift the obfuscating veil that hides ideology's machinations in support of the ruling class. For those using psychoanalytic tools, the goal might be to reveal the motivating desires repressed in the unconscious. But the author of the quote is neither Marxist nor psychoanalyst. Peter Wagner is a Third Wave evangelical. Like social scientific, psychoanalytic, or other forms of academically legitimated methods, spiritual warfare assumes "that reality is more than appears on the surface."[5] But rather than find that reality in the material conditions of existence or in the repressed memories of childhood trauma, spiritual mapping finds the underlying factor to be a supernatural one made up of unseen forces. Wagner writes that "behind many visible aspects of the world around us may be spiritual forces, invisible areas of reality that may have more ultimate significance than the visible."[6] In Third Wave manuals, economic recessions, school shootings, individuals' problems with poverty and addictions, Haiti's social and environmental problems, and Japan's resistance to Christian missionizing are not the result of historical factors and contexts. Rather, people in those countries have taken actions—sometimes wittingly, sometimes not—that have given Satan and his demons legal rights to have control over the physical territory of each country.

The first response from some observers to such supernaturalist explanations is to dismiss them as marginal viewpoints from socially and theologically marginal people: prayers over social actions, the individualization of social problems, the demonization of certain forms of economics, politics, and people.[7] But none of this is much different from late-modern neoliberalism's denial of the powers of history and the existence of the social. And they don't just resemble each other, they are intertwined. Jean Comaroff could well be writing about the Third Wave when she argues that many of the latest developments in contemporary Pentecostalism "are not merely endorsements or 'reflections' of free-market forms: they are reciprocally entailed with economic forces in the thoroughgoing structural reorganization I have identified in the current moment."[8] Like the snare drum that reverberates because of the heavy bass, Third Wave evangelicalism is not merely an inanimate object moved by the forces of sound, but rather a part of neoliberalism's ensemble that fills out the sound. And in this—as well as in its specific engagements with the supernatural, consumerism, therapeutic idioms, globalization, and the notion of atomistic freely willed individuals—it looks like much of the rest of contemporary American religion.

At the same time, a largely unrecognized ambivalence (if there can be such a thing) toward late-modern neoliberalism's ideas resounds in spiritual warfare manuals, and it comes in the form of demons. The sociologist Matthew Wood has suggested that modern possession practices among British New Age practitioners must be understood within the context of "the terms of social conditions of neoliberal globalisation, which ambiguously both removes people from control over their lives while forcing upon them the need to exercise increased control."[9] This is the same with spiritual warfare's demons. In an era in which one prominent view of the individual is that of an agent separable and unaffected by his past and social locations (and always improvable through therapeutic methods), spiritual warfare theologies suggest that evil spirits recurrently torment some people because of past sins that they just can't shake. In a time when we increasingly believe that our identities are achieved rather than ascribed, Third Wave writers declare that one often inherits demons from his ancestors. In a period of accelerated globalization, the exciting possibility of evangelizing the world comes to Third Wave members with a cost: encountering demons associated with other peoples' cultures and religions. And, while many Third Wave writers earnestly proclaim that God prefers free-market capitalism, they also warn that the consumer objects and properties made available by the market frequently house Satan's minions and thus make capitalist consumption potentially perilous to one's soul. Spiritual warfare's battles with demons, played out in the symbolic (and very material) field of Third Wave evangelicalism, suggests a haunting attraction and repulsion toward the very same late-modern social formations from whence it emerged and helps sustain.[10]

NOTES

INTRODUCTION

1 Dan Harris, Jackie Jesko, and Jenna Millman, "Teen Girl Exorcism Squad: Three Arizona Girls Claim to Cast out Demons." *Nightline*, April 5, 2012, http://abcnews.go.com/US/teen-girl-exorcism-squad-arizona-girls-claim-cast/story?id=16074541. Accessed July 13, 2012.

2 Jeff Maysh, "'We're not like Normal Teenagers': Meet the Exorcist Schoolgirls Who Spend Their Time Casting Out Demons around the World." *Daily Mail*, August 11, 2011, http://www.dailymail.co.uk/news/article-2024621/Meet-exorcist-schoolgirls-spend-time-casting-demons-worldwide.html. Accessed June 4, 2012.

3 Nina Rehfeld, "Sie wollen unsere Seelen retten: Diese Teenager treiben uns den Teufel aus." *Glamour* (German Edition) May (2012): 236–239. Thanks to Katja Rakow for pointing me to this source.

4 Charles Pierce, "It Has Come to This: Hot Teen Exorcists." *Esquire Politics Blog*, April 5, 2012, http://www.esquire.com/blogs/politics/teen-exorcists-7865947. Accessed July 13, 2012. For discussion of media coverage from the 1950s to the 1990s, see Sean McCloud, *Making the American Religious Fringe: Exotics, Subversives, and Journalists, 1955–1993* (Chapel Hill: The University of North Carolina Press, 2004).

5 For a discussion of Larson's "tour" with the metal band Slayer (on which he embarked to reveal the satanism behind metal music), see Jason Bivins, *Religion of Fear: The Politics of Horror in Conservative Evangelicalism* (New York: Oxford University Press, 2008), 110–111.

6 While the literature focused on religion and neoliberalism remains small, the multiplication of works on neoliberalism in general continues to grow. For starts, see David Harvey, *A Brief History of Neoliberalism* (New York: Oxford University Press, 2007); Alfredo Saad-Filho and Deborah Johnston (eds), *Neoliberalism: A Critical Reader* (London: Pluto Press, 2005); Carol J. Greenhouse (ed), *Ethnographies of Neoliberalism* (Philadelphia: University of Pennsylvania

Press, 2009); Jean Comaroff and John Comaroff (eds), *Millennial Capitalism and the Culture of Neoliberalism* (Durham, NC: Duke University Press, 2001); and Lisa Duggan, *Twilight of Equality? Neoliberalism, Cultural Politics, and the Attack on Democracy* (Boston: Beacon Press, 2003).

7 Jason Bivins, "'Only One Repertory:' American Religious Studies." *Religion* 42, no. 3 (2012): 395–407. I must note here that I do not see "American religious studies" as something apart from "American religious history." Rather, I see the latter as one approach under the umbrella of the former.

8 Because I have little interest in shoegazing (to here knows when), suffice it to say my vision of American religious studies has little patience for any strongly drawn boundaries that leave out particular theoretical orientations (for example, the frequent preemptive dismissal of psychoanalytic and social theories), subjects (one only has to see the snarky frowns in a room of Americanists when popular culture subjects such as sports, Oprah, or Joel Osteen are mentioned), or approaches (for example, those who think that merely pointing out that an author's approach is "not history" renders her study irrelevant). At the same time, I also have no interest in arguing that the study of American religion needs to expand its boundaries for the sake of inclusiveness that better and more accurately evokes the diversity of the subject. My concern instead lies in the types of questions we ask of our American religious studies topics. It is not what is included and excluded, so much as what we are asking about those things we write about. Though the study of American religion is now ostensibly separated from the seminary, the focus too often still seems to be on narratively answering the descriptive questions of "who," "what," and "when," and much less on those of "how" and "why." But the latter two are the queries that can differentiate our work from that of good journalism. Depending upon what one asks, answering the "hows" and "whys" will call for different—and sometimes combined and interdisciplinary—methods. The field could use some more varied questions, questions that demand attention to language, discourse, embodied habit, the reverberations of institutional structures and material conditions, and the power that all of these things have to enable and constrain religious and scholarly subjects and subjectivities. For an excellent discussion of this issue, see "The Study of American Religions: Critical Reflections on a Specialization" in *Religion* 42, no. 3 (2012): 355–457. The roundtable includes essays by six authors (Jason Bivins, Richard Callahan Jr., Tracy Fessenden, Rosemary Hicks, Kathryn Lofton, and John Lardas Modern) and an introduction by Finbarr Curtis.

9 Lofton, 2. My focus on Third Wave evangelicalism and its relationship with neoliberalism also complements William Connolly's writings on what he calls the "Evangelical-Capitalist Resonance Machine." See his article "The Evangelical-Capitalist Resonance Machine," *Political Theory* 33, no. 6 (2005): 869–886, and

his book *Capitalism and Christianity, American Style.* (Durham, NC: Duke University Press, 2008).

10 See Bivins 2008; and Kelly Baker, *Gospel According to the Klan: The KKK's Appeal to Protestant America, 1915–1930* (Lawrence: University Press of Kansas, 2011). Also see Bill Ellis, *Raising the Devil: Satanism, New Religions, and the Media* (Lexington: University Press of Kentucky, 2000); Bill Ellis, *Lucifer Ascending: The Occult in Folklore and Popular Culture* (Lexington: University Press of Kentucky, 2004); Edward Ingebretson, *Maps of Heaven, Maps of Hell: Religious Terror as Memory from the Puritans to Stephen King* (Armonk, NY: M.E. Sharpe, Inc., 1996); Susan Kwilecki, "Twenty-First-Century American Ghosts: Therapy and Revelation from beyond the Grave," *Religion and American Culture* 19, no. 1 (2009): 101–133; Molly McGarry, *Ghosts of Futures Past: Spiritualism and the Cultural Politics of Nineteenth Century America* (Berkeley: University of California Press, 2008); W. Scott Poole, *Monsters in America: Our Historical Obsession with the Hideous and the Haunting* (Waco, TX: Baylor University Press, 2011); and W. Scott Poole, *Satan in America: The Devil We Know* (Lanham, MD: Rowman and Littlefield, 2010).

11 For more on this, see Sean McCloud. "Hardcore Scholarship and High School Cliques," *Bulletin for the Study of Religion* 41, no. 4 (November 2012): 33–36.

12 With regards to the former, I am increasingly cognizant of the intertwining of differing "fields" of American culture in the contemporary period. Though we use language that addresses subjects such as "religion," "politics," "market," and "popular culture" as if they were easily separable, things don't play out so neatly in the everyday lived practices, habits, and actions of most Americans. The discourse of differentiation, in other words, has limited material affect in everyday life.

13 See Charles Taylor, *A Secular Age* (Cambridge, MA: Belknap/Harvard University Press, 2007); and Steve Bruce, *God is Dead: Secularization in the West* (Malden, MA: Wiley-Blackwell, 2002). For an article that delineates the different meanings of "secularization" in contemporary sociology works and does a good job discussing the confusion the term entails (to which I hope my terse comments here have not added significantly), see David Yamane, "Secularization on Trial: In Defense of a Neo-Secularization Paradigm," *Journal for the Scientific Study of Religion* 36, no. 2 (1997): 107–120.

14 For just one recent example, see Joseph Laycock's argument that the film "*The Exorcist* represents a cultural moment in which the perceived decline of supernaturalism inspired a resurgence in folk piety." See Joseph L. Laycock, "The Folk Piety of Peter Blatty: *The Exorcist* in the Context of Secularization," *Interdisciplinary Journal of Research on Religion* 5, Article 6 (2009), http://www.religjournal.com/articles/article_view.php?id=35. Accessed July 22, 2012.

15 See Tracy Fessenden, *Culture and Redemption: Religion, the Secular, and American Literature* (Princeton, NJ: Princeton University Press, 2006); Winnifred Sullivan, *The Impossibility of Religious Freedom* (Princeton, NJ: Princeton University Press, 2007); John Lardas Modern, *Secularism in Antebellum America* (Chicago: The University of Chicago Press, 2011); Janet Jakobsen and Ann Pellegrini (eds), *Secularisms* (Durham, NC: Duke University Press, 2008); and Janet Jakobsen and Ann Pellegrini, *Love the Sin: Sexual Regulation and the Limits of Religious Tolerance* (Boston: Beacon Press, 2004).

16 Modern, footnote 1 on xvi.

17 See Rene' Holvast, *Spiritual Mapping in the United States and Argentina, 1989–2005* (Boston: Brill, 2009); Thomas Pratt, "The Need to Dialogue: A Review of the Debate on the Controversy of Signs, Wonders, Miracles and Spiritual Warfare Raised in the Literature of the Third Wave Movement," *Pneuma: The Journal of the Society for Pentecostal Studies* 13, no. 1 (1991): 7–32. Bruce Wilson and Rachel Tabachnick, writing for the online religion and politics watchdog site "Talk to Action," have produced a series of essays tracing Third Wave history and figures through their work on one of its subgroups, The New Apostolic Reformation. See, for example, The New Apostolic Reformation Research Team, "Spiritual Mapping and Spiritual Warfare—Muthee and the 'Transformations' Franchise," *Talk to Action,* October 30, 2008, http://www.talk2action.org/story/2008/10/27/115813/98; and Bruce Wilson, "Palin's Churches and the New Apostolic Reformation," *Talk to Action,* September 5, 2008, http://www.talk2action.org/story/2008/9/5/114652/6239. Both accessed July 23, 2012. Wilson and Tabachnick's essays have been reprinted and commented upon in other online journals such as *Huffington Post* and *Religion Dispatches.* For a 2011 NPR *Fresh Air* interview with Rachel Tabachnick on spiritual warfare, see http://www.npr.org/2011/08/24/139781021/the-evangelicals-engaged-in-spiritual-warfare. Accessed July 23, 2012.

18 See Randall Balmer, *Encyclopedia of Evangelicalism* (Louisville, KY: WJK Press, 2002), 576; and Greg Allison, *Historical Theology: An Introduction to Christian Doctrine* (Grand Rapids, MI: Zondervan, 2011), 449.

19 For just four examples, see O'Neill 2010; Amy DeRogatis, "'Born Again is a Sexual Term:' Demons, STDs, and God's Healing Sperm," *Journal of the American Academy of Religion* 77, no. 2 (2009): 275–302; Elizabeth McAlister, "Globalization and the Religious Production of Space," *Journal for the Scientific Study of Religion* 44, no. 3 (2005): 249–255; and Stephen Hunt, "Managing the Demonic: Some Aspects of the Neo-Pentecostal Deliverance Ministry." *Journal of Contemporary Religion* 13, no. 2 (1998): 215–230.

20 See, for example, C. Peter Wagner, "The Third Wave," *Christian Life* (September 1984), np; and C. Peter Wagner, *The Third Wave of the Holy Spirit: Encountering the Power of Signs and Wonders* (Ann Arbor, MI: Vine Books, 1988). George Marsden discusses the controversy of Wagner's and Wimber's

course in his history, *Reforming Fundamentalism: Fuller Seminary and the New Evangelicalism* (Grand Rapids, MI: Eerdmans, 1987), 292–298. See also a record of the discussions, Wagner essays, and the "MC510-Signs, Wonders, and Church Growth" course materials in *Signs and Wonders Today*, compiled by the editors of *Christian Life* magazine (Wheaton, IL: Christian Life Magazine, 1983). In addition to the scholarship cited previously, also see Harvey Cox, *Fire From Heaven: The Rise of Pentecostal Spirituality and the Reshaping of Religion in the Twenty-First Century* (Reading, MA: Addison-Wesley, 1995), 281–285.

21 This is even the case with evangelicals who practice forms of spiritual warfare but disagree with the Third Wave's methods and practice of "strategic-level deliverance." See, for example, James K. Beilby and Paul Rhodes Eddy (eds.), *Understanding Spiritual Warfare: Four Views* (Grand Rapids, MI: Baker Academic, 2012). Bruce Wilson noted this in response to a blog I posted on *Religion in American History,* http://usreligion.blogspot.com/2011/08/protestant-spirits.html. It should also be noted that this book focuses on those forms of spiritual warfare and literature that has direct connections to the Third Wave movement founded by Peter Wagner and his colleagues. These are not the only Christians in the contemporary era who spend time exorcising demons. As seen in work by Thomas Csordas, there remains a small but active Catholic charismatic movement that engages in deliverance ministry. See Thomas Csordas, *The Sacred Self: A Cultural Phenomenology of Charismatic Healing* (Berkeley: University of California Press, 1997). There are also other Protestant charismatics and Pentecostals who practice spiritual warfare, but remain outside the social and institutional networks of the Third Wave. For an overview of demon exorcism in the United States, see Michael Cuneo, *American Exorcism: Expelling Demons in the Land of Plenty* (New York: Broadway Books, 2002). For an example of a work on demon deliverance from a pastor not explicitly connected with the Third Wave networks, see Perry Stone, *Purging Your House, Pruning Your Family Tree: How to Rid Your Home and Family of Demonic Influence and Generational Oppression* (Lakeland, FL: Charisma House, 2011). Demon deliverance handbooks are not an invention of the Third Wave, but predate it. See, for example, Frank and Idae Mae Hammond, *Pigs in the Parlor: The Practical Guide to Deliverance.* (Kirkwood, MO: Impact Books, 1973). For mention of early-twentieth-century Pentecostals and their dealings with demons, see Grant Wacker, *Heaven Below: Early Pentecostals and American Culture.* (Cambridge, MA: Harvard University Press, 2003), 91–92.

22 Cindy Jacobs served on the International Board of Women's Aglow. For Barna's appearance, see George Otis Jr. (director), *The Quickening: Entering into the Firestorm of God's Grace* (Transformations Media, 2003). For Haggard's blurb, see Eddie Smith, *Breaking the Enemy's Grip.* (Minneapolis, MN: Bethany House Publishers, 2004).

23 See Darren Dochuk, *From Bible Belt to Sun Belt: Plain-Folk Religion, Grassroots Politics, and the Rise of Evangelical Conservatism.* (New York: W. W. Norton and Company, 2011).

24 See O'Neill 2010; Holvast 2009; Dan Jorgenson, "Third Wave Evangelism and the Politics of the Global in Papua New Guinea: Spiritual Warfare and the Recreation of Place in Telefolmin," *Oceania* 75(2005): 444–461; and Jean DeBernardini, "Spiritual Warfare and Territorial Spirits: The Globalization and Localization of a 'Practical Theology,'" *Religious Studies and Theology* 18, no. 2 (1999): 66–96. For a Third Wave volume that details some of the missionary interactions with religious "others" and the subsequent development of demonologies, see C. Peter Wagner and F. Douglas Pennoyer (eds), *Wrestling with Dark Angels: Toward a Deeper Understanding of the Supernatural Forces in Spiritual Warfare* (Ventura, CA: Regal Books, 1990).

25 See Dr. Ed Murphy, *The Handbook for Spiritual Warfare.* Revised and Updated. (Nashville: Thomas Nelson Publishers, 2003), 499.

26 See Harold Caballeros, "Defeating the Enemy with the Help of Spiritual Mapping," in *Breaking Strongholds in Your City: How to Use Spiritual Mapping to Make Your Prayers More Strategic, Effective and Targeted*, ed. C. Peter Wagner. (Ventura, CA: Regal Books, 1993), 124.

27 See Murphy 2003, xii.

28 For discussion of the "Satanism scares" of the late 1980s and early 1990s, see Robert Hicks, *In Pursuit of Satan: The Police and the Occult* (Buffalo: Prometheus Books, 1991); James T. Richardson, Joel Best, and David G. Bromley, (eds), *The Satanism Scare* (New York: Aldine De Gruyter, 1991); and Jeffrey Victor, *Satanic Panic: The Creation of a Contemporary Legend* (Chicago: Open Court Press, 1993). For discussion of the Christian Right, see Michael Lienesch, *Redeeming America: Piety and Politics in the New Christian Right* (Chapel Hill: The University of North Carolina Press, 1993); and William Martin, *With God on Our Side: The Rise of the Religious Right in America* (New York: Broadway Books, 2005).

29 See Caballeros 1993, 128.

30 Some handbooks are focused on a single "level," though nearly all guides briefly discuss and define all three levels of spiritual warfare. In brief, authors all argue that ground-level spiritual warfare, in which one works to exile demons tormenting individuals, is the simplest, while strategic-level spiritual warfare, which seeks to expel "territorial spirits" who control large swaths of land, is much more difficult and takes teams of "intercessors" (despite its martial language, Third Wave literature never uses the term "spiritual warriors"), rather than one or a handful of people. See, for example, Rebecca Greenwood's discussion in *Authority to Tread: An Intercessor's Guide to Strategic-Level Spiritual Warfare.* (Grand Rapids, MI: Chosen, 2005).

31 See Walter J. Stephens, *Demon Lovers: Witchcraft, Sex, and the Crisis of Belief* (Chicago: The University of Chicago Press, 2002), 9. For an argument about the importance of demons in the construction of monastic sensibilities, see David Brakke, *Demons and the Making of the Monk: Spiritual Combat in Early Christianity* (Cambridge, MA: Harvard University Press, 2006).

32 An exception to this would be the sociologist Meredith McGuire. Her recent work has focused on individual, "lived" religious practices and critiqued the terms and classifications that social scientists use to poll and analyze Americans as overly institutional, Protestant, and Enlightenment-based. See Meredith McGuire, *Lived Religion: Faith and Practice in Everyday Life* (New York: Oxford University Press, 2008).

33 For discussions of mainline decline, see Richard N. Ostling, "The Church Search," *Time* (April 5, 1993), 44–49; Wade Clark Roof and William McKinney, *American Mainline Religion: Its Changing Shape and Future* (New Brunswick, NJ: Rutgers University Press, 1987); and Robert Wuthnow, *The Restructuring of American Religion* (Princeton, NJ: Princeton University Press, 1988). For discussion of religious "switching," see Wade Clark Roof, *Spiritual Marketplace: Baby Boomers and the Remaking of American Religion* (Princeton, NJ: Princeton University Press, 1999). For discussion of the increase in those identifying themselves as not belonging to any religious group, see Mark Chaves, *American Religion: Contemporary Trends* (Princeton, NJ: Princeton University Press, 2011); and Barry Kosmin, Ariela Keysar, Ryan Cragun, and Juham Navarro-Rivera, "American Nones: The Profile of the No Religion Population" (Hartford, CT: Trinity College, 2009). On religious combining, see Pew Research Center, "Many Americans Mix Multiple Faiths" (np: Pew Forum on Religion and Public Life, 2009). For one of several studies on the high percentage of American who believe in reincarnation, see Humphrey Taylor, "The Religious and Other Beliefs of Americans 2003" (Rochester, NY: Harris Interactive, 2003). In this Harris Poll, 27 percent, responded that they believe in reincarnation (40 percent of those between 25 and 29 years old), even though only about 1–2 percent of all Americans belong to a religious movement that explicitly has this view as part of their tradition's theology. For a discussion of combining as a theme in American religious history, though perhaps one that is more visible today, see Catherine Albanese, "The Culture of Religious Combining: Reflections for the New American Millennium," *Crosscurrents* (Spring/Summer 2000): 16–22. For works that discuss these trends and studies together, see Sean McCloud, "Liminal Subjectivities and Religious Change: Circumscribing Giddens for the Study of American Religion," *Journal of Contemporary Religion* 22, no. 3 (October 2007): 295–309; and Sean McCloud, "Religion and Modern Culture." Bibliographic essay. *CHOICE: Current Reviews for Academic Libraries* (May 2007): 1439–1451.

34 For discussion of these unchanging characteristics of American religion, see McCloud, "Liminal Subjectivities," 298–299.

35 The "dwelling to seeking" description can be found in Robert Wuthnow, *After Heaven: Spirituality in America since the 1950s* (Berkeley: University of California Press, 1998). For "spiritual marketplace," see Roof 1999. For a discussion of the various metaphors and themes that have been used in the ARS subfield of American religious history, see Thomas A. Tweed, "Introduction: Narrating U.S. Religious History." In *Retelling U.S. Religious History*, edited by Thomas A. Tweed (Berkeley: University of California Press, 1997), 1–24.

36 See Lizabeth Cohen, *A Consumer's Republic: The Politics of Mass Consumption in Postwar America* (New York: Vintage Books, 2003).

37 See Cheryl Russell, *The Master Trend: How the Baby Boom Generation Is Remaking America* (New York: Perseus, 1993); and Mara Einstein's discussion of Russell in her *Brands of Faith: Marketing Religion in a Commercial Age* (New York: Routledge, 2008), 10.

38 See Anthony Giddens, *Modernity and Self-Identity: Self and Society in the Late Modern Age.* (Stanford, CA: Stanford University Press, 1991), 198. For discussion of the cultural and identity implications of contemporary work life, see Richard Sennett, *The Corrosion of Character: The Personal Consequences of Work in the New Capitalism* (New York: W.W. Norton and Company, 2000); and Richard Sennett, *The Culture of the New Capitalism* (New Haven, CT: Yale University Press, 2007). For analyses of the changing shape of intimacy, see Eva Illouz, *Why Love Hurts* (Malden, MA: Polity Press, 2012); and Eva Illouz, *Cold Intimacies: The Making of Emotional Capitalism* (Malden, MA: Polity Press, 2007). For a discussion on how social media technologies are changing notions of intimacy, see Sherry Turkle, *Alone Together: Why We Expect More from Technology and Less from Each Other* (New York: Basic Books, 2011).

39 See Wuthnow 1998, 10.

40 See Jeremy Carrette and Richard King, *Selling Spirituality: The Silent Takeover of Religion* (New York: Routledge, 2005), 44.

41 See Roof 1999. For discussion of "deculturing" religions, see Olivier Roy 2010. For a volume on religion and consumerism, see Francois Gauthier and Tuomas Martikainen (eds), *Religion in Consumer Society: Brands, Consumers, and Markets* (Burlington, VT: Ashgate, 2013).

42 See Einstein 2008.

43 See Andrew McKinnon, "Ideology and the Market Metaphor in Rational Choice Theory of Religion: A Rhetorical Critique of 'Religious Economies,'" *Critical Sociology* 39 (July 2013): 529–543.

44 For an example from the sociology of religion, see Rodney Stark and Roger Finke, *Acts of Faith: Explaining the Human Side of Religion* (Berkeley: University of California Press, 2000). For an example from journalism, see Richard

Cimino and Don Lattin, *Shopping for Faith: American Religion in the New Millennium* (San Francisco: Jossey-Bass, 1998).

45 Brad Gregory, *The Unintended Reformation: How a Religious Revolution Secularized Society* (Cambridge, MA: Belknap/Harvard University Press, 2012), 236, 237.

46 Lofton 2011, 10.

47 See Bethany Moreton, *To Serve God and Wal-Mart: The Making of Christian Free Enterprise* (Cambridge, MA: Harvard University Press, 2009); Bethany Moreton, "The Soul of Neoliberalism," *Social Text* 92 25, no. 3 (Fall 2007): 104–123; Stefania Palmisano, "New Monasticism and the Consumer Economy: A Paradox?" Paper presentation at SOCREL Study Group of the British Sociological Association (March 2012); Michael Brown, *The Channeling Zone: American Spirituality in an Anxious Age* (Cambridge, MA: Harvard University Press, 1997); Courtney Bender, *The New Metaphysicals: Spirituality and the American Religious Imagination* (Chicago: The University of Chicago Press, 2010); and Hugh Urban, "Avatar for Our Age: Sathya Sai Baba and the Cultural Contradictions of Late Capitalism," *Religion* 33(2003): 73–93.

48 A search on Amazon.com on August 4, 2012, found 363 items available under the moniker "ghost hunting equipment," including complete kits ranging from $99.95 to $279.95. For the poll suggesting 32 percent, see Linda Lyons, "One-Third of Americans Believe Dearly May not Have Departed," *Gallup* (July 12, 2005), http://www.gallup.com/poll/17275/onethird-americans-believe-dearly-may-departed.aspx. Accessed August 4, 2012. For two examples suggesting that the number is closer to half, see Christopher D. Bader, F. Carson Mencken, and Joseph O. Baker, *Paranormal America: Ghost Encounters, UFO Sightings, Bigfoot Hunts, and Other Curiosities in Religion and Culture* (New York: New York University Press, 2010), 44; and Sean Alfano, "Poll: The Majority Believe in Ghosts." *CBS News Online* (February 11, 2009): http://www.cbsnews.com/stories/2005/10/29/opinion/polls/main994766.shtml. Accessed August 4, 2012. While polls don't reveal whether the trends they mark are new or whether people are just answering more honestly (or dishonestly), either way suggests a change in attitude. Also see the 2007 Pew "U.S. Religious Landscape Survey," http://pewresearch.org/databank/dailynumber/?NumberID=885. Accessed August 4, 2012.

49 Conversation with Jason Bivins.

50 For discussion about religion—specifically Roman Catholicism and Wicca— and its role in *Paranormal State*, see Ryan Buell and Stefan Petrucha, *Paranormal State: My Journey into the Unknown* (New York: HarperCollins Publishers, 2010). For an example of religion in the series *A Haunting*, see the 2006 episode "The Unleashed" (available via Youtube, http://www.youtube.com/watch?v=JkRfhNF5by8. Accessed August 4, 2012.) With a combination of

actors and interviews, it recounts the story of Randy Ervin, who becomes tormented by demons in rural Standish, Michigan, in the mid-1970s. The episode follows the typical chronological trajectory of most evangelical narratives about individuals who move from "occultism" to evangelicalism. It also features elements found in many contemporary horror films. Ervin moves into a home built on an Indian burial ground (he finds bones in the basement) and begins experiencing strange phenomena, including seeing dark shadows and having lights and radios turn on by themselves. His curiosity leads him to the public library, where he checks out a book of spells and begins "dabbling in the occult" by performing rituals. This "invites" demons into his home and life, resulting in much hardship. He seeks help from a minister (liberal Protestant?), who tells him there are no such things as demons. He then asks a "white witch" to come to his home and banish the evil spirits, but this action merely brings more torment. The horror ends when Ervin is introduced to a beautician who is also a lay deliverance minister. She asks Randy to give his heart to Jesus, evicts the resistant demons residing within him through prayer and a large cross, and later blesses his home. The episode ends with Ervin warning viewers not to dabble in the occult and witchcraft, because "it will open a door you cannot close." While not all episodes of *A Haunting* feature such explicit evangelical plots, many involve Roman Catholic and evangelical elements. For a discussion of the influence of evangelicalism in contemporary horror media, see Lynn Schofield Clark's chapter "Angels, Aliens, and the Dark Side of Evangelicalism" in her book *From Angels to Aliens: Teenagers, the Media, and the Supernatural* (New York: Oxford University Press, 2003), 24–45. Also see Bivins 2008 and Ingebretson 1996.

[51] For the autobiography and "how-to" manual of the primary figure in *Psychic Kids: Children of the Paranormal*, see Chip Coffey, *Growing up Psychic* (New York: Three Rivers Press, 2012).

[52] One exception to these characterizations is the preponderance of investigations of open and working museums and historical sites on the SYFY channel series *Ghosthunters*. Their visits have included the National Baseball Hall of Fame, the Mark Twain House, and numerous fort and lighthouse museums/attractions. One wonders if the neoliberal era of reduced government funding for such places has made the presence of a ghost—and the tourists who want to see it—vital to keeping some historical institutions open.

[53] Both of these examples come from episodes of *Paranormal State*. See "Dead and Back" (episode 51, season 3, May 11, 2009) and "Spirits of the Slave Dungeon" (episode 67, season 5, October 24, 2010).

[54] See Sigmund Freud, *The Uncanny* (New York: Penguin Classics, 2003), 148.

[55] See Judith Richardson, *Possessions: The History and Uses of Haunting in the Hudson Valley* (Cambridge, MA: Harvard University Press, 2003), 3. Also see Avery Gordon, *Ghostly Matters: Haunting and the Sociological Imagination* (Minneapolis: University of Minnesota Press, 1997).

56 For works on the therapeutic discourse, see Phillip Rief, *Triumph of the Therapeutic: Uses of Faith after Freud* (New York: Harper and Row, 1966); Jonathan Imber (ed), *Therapeutic Culture: Triumph and Defeat* (Piscataway, NJ: Transaction Publishers, 2004); and Frank Furedi, *Therapy Culture: Cultivating Vulnerability in an Uncertain Age* (New York: Routledge, 2003). See Eva Illouz, *Saving the Modern Soul: Therapy, Emotions, and the Culture of Self-Help* (Berkeley: University of California Press, 2008), 243.

57 See Brown 1997; Bender 2010; Joseph Tamney, *The Resilience of Conservative Religion: The Case of Popular, Conservative Congregations* (New York: Cambridge University Press, 2002); Kimon Howland Sargeant, *Seeker Churches: Promoting Traditional Religion in a Nontraditional Way* (Piscataway, NJ: Rutgers University Press, 2000); E. Brooks Holifield, *A History of Pastoral Care in America: From Salvation to Self-Realization* (Nashville, TN: Abingdon Press, 1983); Janice Peck, *The Age of Oprah: Cultural Icon for the Neoliberal Era* (Boulder, CO: Paradigm Publishers, 2008); and Lofton 2011. See Holifield 1983; Joel Osteen, *Your Best Life Now: 7 Steps to Living at Your Full Potential* (New York: Faithwords, 2004); Rick Warren, *The Purpose Driven Life* (Grand Rapids, MI: Zondervan, 2002); and Rick Warren, *The Purpose Driven Life Journal* (Grand Rapids, MI: Zondervan, 2002). See Phillip Hammond, *Religion and Personal Autonomy: The Third Disestablishment in America* (Columbia: South Carolina University Press, 1992).

58 For a useful discussion about truth claims in an era in which we have moved from "consensus reality to virtual reality" (page 8), see Jodi Dean, *Aliens in America: Conspiracy Cultures from Outerspace to Cyberspace* (Ithaca, NY: Cornell University Press, 1998).

CHAPTER ONE

1 Cindy Jacobs, *Deliver Us from Evil: Putting a Stop to the Occultic Influence Invading your Home and Community* (Ventura, CA: Regal Books, 2001), 18.

2 In the forward to Jacobs's Reformation Manifesto, Wagner asserts that the Second Apostolic Age began in 2001 and is the "greatest change in the ways of doing church at least since the Protestant Reformation." See Cindy Jacobs, *The Reformation Manifesto* (Minneapolis, MN: Bethany House Publishers, 2008), 9, 10. For one description of the three levels of spiritual warfare, see Rebecca Greenwood, *Authority to Tread: An Intercessor's Guide to Strategic Level Spiritual Warfare* (Grand Rapids, MI: Chosen, 2005), 21–26.

3 The historian of science Bruno Latour suggests that modernity is characterized by, first, "translation," which consists of practices that create "mixtures between entirely new types of beings, hybrids of nature and culture," and, second, the work of purification, which seeks to partition the world into categories of human/

nonhuman, nature/culture. Bruno Latour, *We Have Never Been Modern*. Translated by Catherine Porter (Cambridge, MA: Harvard University Press, 1993), 10–11; Webb Keane, *Christian Moderns: Freedom and Fetish in the Mission Encounter* (Berkeley: University of California Press, 2007), 77. See Latour 1993, 12.

4   Jason Bivins, *Religion of Fear: The Politics of Horror in Conservative Evangelicalism* (New York: Oxford University Press, 2008), 17–18. While Bivins's focus on politically oriented conservative evangelicals in *Fear* is more expansive than mine here on the Third Wave, there is of course much overlap of individuals and institutions. As I note later in this chapter, the Third Wave is to conservative evangelicalism what the Tea Party is to the Republican Party. For two other useful studies that focus on the projection, internalization, and mimicry of the "other" within demonologies, see Bill Ellis, *Raising the Devil: Satanism, New Religions, and the Media* (Lexington: University Press of Kentucky, 2000); and David Frankfurter, *Evil Incarnate: Rumors of Demonic Conspiracy and Satanic Abuse in History* (Princeton, NJ: Princeton University Press, 2006).

5   For a useful discussion of imagined threats to youth, see Sarah Pike, "Dark Teens and Born-Again Martyrs: Captivity Narratives After Columbine," *Journal of the American Academy of Religion* 77, no. 3 (2009): 647–679.

6   C. Peter Wagner, *The Third Wave of the Holy Spirit: Encountering the Power of Signs and Wonders* (Ann Arbor, MI: Vine Books, 1988), 85, 86.

7   See Harold Caballeros, *Victorious Warfare: Discovering your Rightful Place in God's Kingdom* (Nashville, TN: Thomas Nelson Publishers, 2001), 87; and Rebecca Greenwood, *Authority to Tread: An Intercessor's Guide to Strategic Level Spiritual Warfare* (Grand Rapids, MI: Chosen, 2005), 43.

8   See Diana Eck, *A New Religious America: How a "Christian Country" has become the World's Most Religiously Diverse Nation* (San Francisco: HarperSanFrancisco, 2002); William R. Hutchison, *Religious Pluralism in America: The Contentious History of a Founding Ideal* (Hartford, CN: Yale University Press, 2004); Stephen Prothero (ed.), *A Nation of Religions: The Politics of Pluralism in Multireligious America* (Chapel Hill: The University of North Carolina Press, 2006); Courtney Bender and Pamela Klassen (eds.), *After Pluralism: Reimagining Religious Engagement* (New York: Columbia University Press, 2010); and Charles L. Cohen and Ronald L. Numbers (eds.), *Gods in America: Religious Pluralism in the United States* (New York: Oxford University Press, 2013).

9   Ed Murphy, *The Handbook for Spiritual Warfare*. Revised and updated (Nashville: Thomas Nelson Publishers, 2003), 182. For the Thai Buddhist temple demons and Rudra, the Indian storm god, see C. Peter Wagner, *Warfare Prayer: How to Seek God's Power and Protection in the Battle to Build His Kingdom* (Ventura, CA: Regal Books, 1992), 76, 143. For a prayer against a Muslim temple being built, see Cindy Jacobs, *Possessing the Gates of the Enemy: A Training Manual for Militant Intercession*. Second edition with study guide

(Grand Rapids, MI: Baker Books, 1994), 48–49. For the comment on the Talmud as superstitious, see George Otis Jr., *Informed Intercession* (Ventura, CA: Renew Books, 1999), 200. For the warning to pray against Hindu demons, see Rebecca Greenwood, *Let Our Children Go: Steps to Free Your Child from Evil Influences and Demonic Harassment*. (Lake Mary, FL: Charisma House, 2011), 29.

10 For a discussion of evangelical anti-cult literature from the 1950s to the 1990s, see Sean McCloud, *Making the American Religious Fringe: Exotics, Subversives, and Journalists, 1955–1993* (Chapel Hill: The University of North Carolina Press, 2004). See John Higham, *Strangers in the Land: Patterns of American Nativism, 1860–1925* (New Brunswick, NJ: Rutgers University Press, 2002); Jenny Franchot, *Roads to Rome: The Antebellum Protestant Encounter with Catholicism* (Berkeley: University of California Press, 1994); and John Corrigan and Lynn S. Neal, eds., *Religious Intolerance in America: A Documentary History* (Chapel Hill: The University of North Carolina Press, 2010).

11 For the 1647 Puritan law banning Jesuits from the Massachusetts Bay Colony, see Richard S. Dunn (ed.), *The Laws and Liberties of Massachusetts: Reprinted from the Unique Copy of the 1648 Edition in the Henry E. Huntington Library* (Cambridge: Huntington Library Press, 1998). For an example of anti-Catholic antebellum literature, see Maria Monk, *The Awful Disclosures of Maria Monk* (London: Houlston and Stoneman, 1851). For an examination of early-twentieth-century Klan anti-Catholicism, see Lynn S. Neal, "Christianizing the Klan: Alma White, Branford Clarke, and the Art of Religious Intolerance," *Church History* 78, no. 2 (June 2009): 350–378. The flyer from the Denver, North Carolina, Pentecostal church was shown to me by a student taking one of my courses. See Michael Lienesch, *Redeeming America: Piety and Politics in the New Christian Right* (Chapel Hill: The University of North Carolina Press, 1993); William Martin, *With God on Our Side: The Rise of the Religious Right in America* (New York: Broadway Books, 2005); and Seth Dowland, "'Family' Values and the Formation of a Christian Right Agenda." *Church History* 78, no. 3 (September 2009): 606–631.

12 Eddie Smith and Alice Smith, *Spiritual House Cleaning: Protect Your Home and Family From Spiritual Pollution* (Ventura, CA: Regal Books, 2003), 50.

13 For some examples of imagining Jesus in America, see Stephen Prothero, *American Jesus: How the Son of God Became a National Icon* (New York: Farrar, Straus, and Giroux, 2003); Richard Wightman Fox, *Jesus in America: Personal Savior, Cultural Hero, National Obsession* (San Francisco: HarperOne, 2004); and Edward J. Blum and Paul Harvey, *The Color of Christ: The Son of God and the Saga of Race in America*. (Chapel Hill: The University of North Carolina Press, 2012). See David Morgan, Visual Piety: A *History and Theory of Popular Religious Images* (Berkeley: University of California Press, 1998), 112–115.

14   Cindy Jacobs, *Deliver Us from Evil: Putting a Stop to the Occultic Influence Invading your Home and Community* (Ventura, CA: Regal Books, 2001), 213.

15   See Andrew Chestnut, *Devoted to Death: Santa Muerte, the Skeleton Saint* (New York: Oxford University Press, 2012). C. Peter Wagner, *Warfare Prayer: How to Seek God's Power and Protection in the Battle to Build His Kingdom* (Ventura, CA: Regal Books, 1992), 34.

16   See C. Peter Wagner, *Confronting the Queen of Heaven* (Pasadena, CA: Wagner Institute Publications, 2001).

17   Rebecca Greenwood, *Authority to Tread: An Intercessor's Guide to Strategic-Level Spiritual Warfare* (Grand Rapids, MI: Chosen, 2005), 45, 47, 48, 49. For the story of Santa Maria Maggiore Church in Rome and the Monastery of the Caves in Kiev, see 51–53 and 63 and Appendix D.

18   Wagner 1992, 28.

19   Ed Murphy, *The Handbook for Spiritual Warfare*. Revised and updated (Nashville: Thomas Nelson Publishers, 2003), 179.

20   F. Douglas Pennoyer, "In Dark Dungeons of Collective Captivity," in *Wrestling with Dark Angels: Toward a Deeper Understanding of the Supernatural Forces in Spiritual Warfare*, ed. C. Peter Wagner and F. Douglas Pennoyer (Ventura, CA: Regal Books, 1990), 256–257.

21   Murphy 2003, 179.

22   For one example of cultural critique, see the fundamentalists featured in George Marsden, *Fundamentalism and American Culture: The Shaping of Twentieth Century Evangelicalism, 1870–1925* (New York: Oxford University Press, 1980). This is correct, though I believe the newest edition skips the subtitle The historian Grant Wacker has argued that Pentecostals embraced various pragmatic and "modern" technologies and styles while simultaneously exhibiting an otherworldly idealism. Grant Wacker, *Heaven Below: Early Pentecostals and American Culture.* (Cambridge,, MA: Harvard University Press, 2001). For examples of conservative Protestants embracing new media technologies, see Tona Hangen, *Redeeming the Dial: Radio, Religion, and Popular Culture in America* (Chapel Hill: The University of North Carolina Press, 2001); and Heather Hendersot, *Shaking the World for Jesus: Media and Conservative Evangelical Culture* (Chicago: University of Chicago Press, 2004). For examples of conservative Protestant embrace of American popular-music styles, see Eileen Luhr, "Punk, Metal, and American Religions." *Religion Compass* 4, no. 7 (2010): 443–451; and David Stowe, *No Sympathy for the Devil: Christian Pop Music and the Transformation of American Evangelicalism* (Chapel Hill: The University of North Carolina Press, 2011).

23   Lynne Gerber, *Seeking the Straight and Narrow: Weight Loss and Sexual Reorientation in Evangelical America*(Chicago: The University of Chicago Press, 2012), 6.

24 Rebecca Greenwood, *Breaking the Bonds of Evil: How to Set People Free from Demonic Oppression* (Grand Rapids, MI: Chosen, 2006), 74.

25 In this way, Third Wave attitudes toward heavy metal and extreme music mirror those of some in the broader evangelical culture. See Jason Bivins 2008.

26 For an excellent discussion of evangelical theories of backward masking, see Jacob Smith, "Turn Me On, Dead Media: A Backward Look at the Re-Enchantment of an Old Medium," *Television and New Media* 12, no. 6 (2011): 531–551. For the description of demons' voices on recordings, see Smith, 539. Unlike the PMRC, spiritual warfare handbooks give little to no mention of hip-hop and rap.

27 Greenwood, *Authority to Tread*, 25.

28 Greenwood 2011, 56, 131, 135. Jacobs 2001, 172–174.

29 See, for example, Wagner's interview on National Public Radio's *Fresh Air with Terry Gross*. While Wagner said he believed that "there's a lot of demonic control over Congress in general that needs to be dispersed," he was hesitant in this media venue to point out the Democratic Party as particularly demonized, as did his New Apostolic Reformation colleague Alice Patterson. For the interview, see http://www.npr.org/2011/10/03/140946482/apostolic-leader-weighs-religions-role-in-politics. Accessed 5/6/2013.

30 Jacobs 2008, 19. Patterson 2010, 197. Jacobs 2001, 66. Patterson 2010, 217.

31 See, for example, Kyle Mantyla, "Rick Perry, Alice Patterson, and the Demons who Control our Politics." *Right Wing Watch* (August 12, 2011). http://www.rightwingwatch.org/content/rick-perry-alice-patterson-and-demons-who-control-our-politics. Accessed 9 May 2013.

32 See the Justice at the Gate website: http://www.justiceatthegate.org/Default.asp. Accessed May 9, 2013.

33 Patterson 2010, 145, 152, 157, 191.

34 Patterson 2010, 193, 200, 201, 202.

35 William E. Connolly, "The Evangelical-Capitalist Resonance Machine," *Political Theory* 33, no. 6 (2005): 869–886; and *Capitalism and Christianity, American Style*. (Durham, NC: Duke University Press, 2008).

36 Cindy Jacobs, "Dealing with Strongholds," in *Breaking Strongholds in Your City: How to Use Spiritual Mapping to Make Your Prayers More Strategic, Effective and Targeted*, ed. C. Peter Wagner (Ventura, CA: Regal Books, 1993), 85.

37 Murphy 2003, 500.

38 See David Brion Davis, "Some Themes of Countersubversion: An Analysis of Anti-Masonic, Anti-Catholic, and Anti-Mormon Literature," *The Mississippi Valley Historical Review* (September 1960): 205–224; Michael Barkun, *A Culture of Conspiracy: Apocalyptic Visions in Contemporary America*, (Berkeley: University of California Press, 2006); Richard Hofstadter, *The Paranoid Style in American Politics* (New York: Vintage, 2008); and John

Higham, *Strangers in the Land: Patterns in American Nativism, 1860–1925* (New Brunswick: NJ: Rutgers University Press, 2002).

39 For a useful academic definition of "occult," see Robert Galbreath, "Explaining Modern Occultism," in *The Occult in America: New Historical Perspectives*, ed. Howard Kerr and Charles L. Crow. (Urbana: University of Illinois Press, 1983), 11–37.

40 Greenwood 2006, 84, 89, 90.

41 Barry Kosmin, Egon Mayer, and Ariela Keysar, "American Religious Identification Survey 2001" (New York: The Graduate Center of the City University of New York, 2001).

42 For a study examining the attraction of Wicca to some teens, see Helen Berger and Douglas Ezzy, *Teenage Witches: Magical Youth and the Search for the Self* (New Brunswick, NJ: Rutgers University, 2007). Greenwood 2006, 52.

43 Murphy 2003, 499.

44 For just a few works, see Bill Ellis, *Raising the Devil: Satanism, New Religions, and the Media* (Lexington: University Press of Kentucky, 2000); Frankfurter 2006; Robert Hicks, *In Pursuit of Satan: The Police and the Occult* (Buffalo: Prometheus Books, 1991); James T. Richardson, Joel Best, and David G. Bromley, ed., *The Satanism Scare* (New York: Aldine De Gruyter, 1991); and Jeffrey Victor, *Satanic Panic: The Creation of a Contemporary Legend* (Chicago: Open Court Press, 1993).

45 Jacobs 2001, 153, 169, 166.

46 Gary Alan Fine and Patricia A. Turner, *Whispers on the Color Line: Rumor and Race in America* (Berkeley: University of California Press, 2004). Also see Gary Alan Fine, *Manufacturing Tales: Sex, Money, Contemporary Legends* (Knoxville: University of Tennessee Press, 1992); and Jan Brunvand, *The Vanishing Hitchhiker: American Urban Legends and their Meanings* (New York: W.W. Norton and Company, 1981).

47 Harold Caballeros, *Victorious Warfare: Discovering Your Rightful Place in God's Kingdom* (Nashville, TN: Thomas Nelson Publishers, 2001), 24.

48 For two studies of demons in Christianity, see David Brakke, *Demons and the Making of the Monk: Spiritual Combat in Early Christianity* (Cambridge, MA: Harvard University Press, 2006); and Walter Stephens, *Demon Lovers: Witchcraft, Sex, and the Crisis of Belief* (Chicago: The University of Chicago Press, 2002). For mention of early-twentieth-century Pentecostals and their dealings with demons, see Wacker, *Heaven Below*, 91–92.

49 For a study of ghost reality television, see Annette Hill, *Paranormal Media: Audiences, Spirits and Magic in Popular Culture* (New York: Routledge, 2010).

50 In phrasing it like this, I am making a distinction between elements that are part of religious social formations (Jesus, "born-again" conversion experiences) and motifs and themes that have no direct connection to specific religious movements

(ghosts). At the same time, I don't think it is useful, as a scholar, to distinguish "religious" from "nonreligious" supernatural themes and elements. Such boundaries are often based on conventional and institutional definitions of religion and fail to recognize that one could as easily recognize any supernatural motif/narrative as being "religious." Such boundary marking depends upon subjective definitions of religion, which are more interesting and useful for scholars to analyze than engage in.

51 Patterson 2010, 148.

52 Greenwood 2011, 13.

53 For the quotations, see Greenwood 2011, 15. Third Wave authors Alice and Eddie Smith suggest that children can see angels and demons. They recount a story in which their fourteen-year-old son reports seeing hundreds of demonic faces on his bedroom ceiling at night. He prayed to God to get rid of the faces, but God declined, telling the teen that he wanted the demons to have to watch the boy sleep. "Can you imagine the humiliation," write the Smiths, "experienced by a team of demons whose only job was to scare a young servant of the Lord as they watched him peacefully fall asleep amid their threats?" Eddie and Alice Smith, *Spiritual House Cleaning*, 41. *Psychic Kids: Children of the Paranormal* is a particularly rich example of a ghost reality show that elaborates common folk/popular ideas about children and the supernatural. Chip Coffey, a psychic who features prominently in the program, has written a semi-autobiographical manual to assist "psychic children" that also contains these prominent motifs. See Chip Coffey, *Growing up Psychic* (New York: Three Rivers Press, 2012).

54 Jacobs 2001, 199. For Third Wave discussion of shapeshifting and astral projection, see Jacobs 2001, 87 and 130. In the same volume, Jacobs suggests—as do other spiritual warfare manual writers—that one must be careful when coming across a "Satanic altar." She asserts that powerful curses placed in the altars can harm those who "presumptuously destroy them." "I have known intercessors," she writes, "who moved in presumption and then saw their families fall apart, got divorced or were financially ruined." Jacobs 2001, 169.

55 George Otis Jr., *Informed Intercession* (Ventura, CA: Renew Books, 1999), 199; Eddie and Alice Smith, Spiritual House Cleaning, 10.

56 Ellis 2000, Bivins 2008, and Frankfurter 2006.

57 Otis, Jr. 2003, 163–167.

58 See, for example, Alma White, *Demons and Tongues* (Zarephath, NJ: Pillar of Fire Publishers, 1949).

59 See Richard Godbeer, *The Devil's Dominion: Magic and Religion in Early New England* (New York: Cambridge University Press, 1992); David D. Hall, *Worlds of Wonder, Days of Judgment: Popular Religious Belief in Early New England* (Cambridge, MA: Harvard University Press, 1990); David D. Hall, ed., *Witch-Hunting in Seventeenth-Century New England: A Documentary History*

1638–1693. Second Edition (Durham, NC: Duke University Press, 2005); and Jon Butler, *Awash in a Sea of Faith: Christianizing the American People* (Cambridge, MA: Harvard University Press, 1992).

60 Richard Twiss, One Church, *Many Tribes: Following Jesus the Way God Made You* (Ventura, CA: Regal Books, 2003), 82–83.

61 Twiss 2003, 95, 112, 127.

62 Walter Wink and Michael Hardin, "Response to C. Peter Wagner and Rebecca Greenwood," in *Understanding Spiritual Warfare: Four Views*, ed. James K. Beilby and Paul Rhodes Eddy (Grand Rapids, MI: Baker Academic, 2012), 203. David Powlison, "Response to C. Peter Wagner and Rebecca Greenwood." In Understanding Spiritual Warfare, 204.

63 For studies that examine the meanings and usages of "syncretism," "hybrid," "creole," and "combinative," see Deborah A. Kapchan and Pauline Turner Strong, "Theorizing the Hybrid," *Journal of American Folklore* 112, no. 445 (Summer 1999): 239–253; Anita Maria Leopold and Jeppe Sinding Jensen (eds.), *Syncretism in Religion: A Reader* (New York: Routledge, 2004); Joel Robbins, "Crypto-Religion and the Study of Cultural Mixes: Anthropology, Value, and the Nature of Syncretism," *Journal of the American Academy of Religion* 79, no. 2 (June 2011): 408–424; Rosiland Shaw and Charles Stewart (eds.), *Syncretism/Anti-Syncretism: The Politics of Religious Synthesis* (New York: Routledge, 1994), and Charles Stewart, "Syncretism and Its Synonyms: Reflections on Cultural Mixture," *Diacritics* 29, no. 3 (Fall 1999): 40–62.

CHAPTER TWO

1 "Mark" is a pseudonym.

2 Daniel Miller, *The Comfort of Things* (Malden, MA: Polity Press, 2008), 91; Colin Campbell, "Romanticism and the Consumer Ethic: Intimations of a Weber-Style Thesis," *Sociological Analysis* 44, no. 4 (Winter 1983): 279–295; Anthony Giddens, *Modernity and Self-Identity: Self and Society in the Late Modern Age* (Stanford, CA: Stanford University Press, 1991), 196, 198.

3 Jeremy Biles, "Out of this World: The Materiality of the Beyond," in *Religion and Material Culture: The Matter of Belief*, ed. David Morgan (New York: Routledge, 2010), 139.

4 Harold Caballeros, *Victorious Warfare: Discovering Your Rightful Place in God's Kingdom* (Nashville, TN: Thomas Nelson Publishers, 2001), 79.

5 Eddie Smith and Alice Smith. *Spiritual Housecleaning: Protect Your Home and Family From Spiritual Pollution* (Ventura, CA: Regal Books, 2003); and Chuck D. Pierce and Rebecca Wagner Systema, *Protecting Your Home from Spiritual Darkness* (Ventura, CA: Regal Books, 2004). While Pierce and Systema are both listed as authors of *Protecting Your Home from Spiritual Darkness*, I

often use Pierce's name singularly in the text because he narrates all of my examples and quotations from the volume in the first person. Eddie and Alice Smith 2003, 44; Pierce and Systema 2004, 20.

6   Cindy Jacobs, *Deliver Us from Evil: Putting a Stop to the Occultic Influence Invading Your Home and Community* (Ventura, CA: Regal Books, 2001), 198; and Harold Caballeros, *Victorious Warfare: Discovering your Rightful Place in God's Kingdom* (Nashville, TN: Thomas Nelson Publishers, 2001), 82–83.

7   Amy Whitehead, "The Goddess and the Virgin: Materiality in Western Europe," *The Pomegranate* 10, no. 2 (2008): 164. In addition to Whitehead, see Nicole Boivin, "Grasping the Elusive and Unknowable: Material Culture in Ritual Practice," *Material Religion* 5, no. 3 (2009): 266–287; and Peter Pels, "The Modern Fear of Matter: Reflections on the Protestantism of Victorian Science," *Material Religion* 4, no. 3 (2008): 264–283.

8   Eddie and Alice Smith 2003, 10; Pierce and Systema 2004, 21.

9   Eddie and Alice Smith 2003, 25; Pierce and Systema 2004, 33. Regarding rosary beads and crucifixes, see Eddie and Alice Smith, 49–52.

10 Eddie and Alice Smith 2003, 62, 63, 30, 30–31.

11 Pierce and Systema 2004, 80. In the same volume, Chuck Pierce tells a very similar story about a Magic 8 Ball toy. When his other son buys the toy, Pierce tells him it is evil, but isn't believed. Pierce then prays than his son "Isaac would see the demonic force behind the object"; in a few days, Isaac does, and the family ritually destroys the toy together. Pierce and Systema 2004, 80–81.

12 Pierce and Systema 2004, 26.

13 Pierce and Systema 2004, 27.

14 George Otis Jr., *Informed Intercession: Transforming Your Community Through Spiritual Mapping and Strategic Prayer* (Ventura, CA: Renew Books, 1999), 174.

15 Eddie and Alice Smith 2003, 35; Jeffrey Sconce, *Haunted Media: Electronic Presence from Telegraphy to Television* (Durham, NC: Duke University Press, 2000); Pierce and Systema 2004, 22, 23.

16 C. Peter Wagner, *The Third Wave of the Holy Spirit: Encountering the Power of Signs and Wonders* (Ann Arbor, MI: Vine Books, 1988), 64.

17 Wagner 1988, 65, 66, 67.

18 Pierce and Systema 2004, 48.

19 Eddie and Alice Smith 2003, 57–58.

20 Eddie and Alice Smith 2003, 76, 48; Pierce and Systema 2004, 24.

21 Eddie and Alice Smith 2003, 75, 35, 55; Pierce and Systema 2004, 49–50, 52, 56.

22 Pierce and Systema 2004, 52; Eddie and Alice Smith 2003, 46–47.

23 Bob Beckett, "Practical Steps Toward Community Deliverance," in *Breaking Strongholds in Your City: How to Use Spiritual Mapping to Make Your Prayers More Strategic, Effective and Targeted*, ed. C. Peter Wagner (Ventura, CA: Regal Books, 1993), 148, 153.

24 Beckett 1993, 150, 151.

25 Renee L. Bergland, *The National Uncanny: Indian Ghosts and American Subjects* (Hanover, NH: Dartmouth College Press, 2000); Robert F. Berkhofer Jr., *The White Man's Indian: Images of the American Indian from Columbus to the Present* (New York: Vintage Books, 1978); *Radical Spirits: Spiritualism and Women's Rights in Nineteenth-Century America* (Boston: Beacon Press, 1989); and Molly McGarry, *Ghosts of Futures Past: Spiritualism and the Cultural Politics of Nineteenth-Century America* (Berkeley: University of California Press, 2008).

26 Pierce and Systema 2004, 55.

27 Charles Berlitz, *The Bermuda Triangle* (New York: Doubleday, 1974); C. Peter Wagner, "Territorial Spirits," in *Wrestling with Dark Angels: Toward a Deeper Understanding of the Supernatural Forces in Spiritual Warfare*, ed. C. Peter Wagner and F. Douglas Pennoyer (Ventura, CA: Regal Books, 1990), 83.

28 Jeffrey Weinstock, "Introduction: The Spectral Turn," in *Spectral America: Phantoms and the National Imagination*, ed. Jeffrey Weinstock (Madison, WI: University of Wisconsin Press, 2004), 6.

29 Kjell Sjoberg, "Spiritual Mapping for Prophetic Prayer Actions," in *Breaking Strongholds in Your City*, 117–118. Cindy Jacobs, *Possessing the Gates of the Enemy: A Training Manual for Militant Intercession*. Second edition with study guide (Grand Rapids, MI: Baker Books, 1994), 36–37.

30 Timothy Cresswell, *Place: A Short Introduction* (Malden, MA: Blackwell, 2004), 27.

31 Matthew Glass, "'Alexanders All:' Symbols of Conquest and Resistance at Mount Rushmore," in *American Sacred Space*, ed. David Chidester and Edward Linenthal (Bloomington: Indiana University Press, 1995), 156.

32 Pierce and Systema 2004, 66.

33 Pierce and Systema 2004, 55; Eddie and Alice Smith 2003, 76, 55, 35.

34 Kevin Lewis O'Neill, *City of God: Christian Citizenship in Postwar Guatemala* (Berkeley: University of California Press, 2010); Michael O. Emerson and Christian Smith, *Divided by Faith: Evangelical Religion and the Problem of Race in America* (New York: Oxford University Press, 2000).

35 Pierce and Systema 2004, 56; Beckett 1993, 166–167; Pierce and Systema 2004, 92.

36 E. C. Relph, *Place and Placelessness* (London: Pion, 1976), 39.

37 Mircea Eliade, *The Sacred and the Profane: The Nature of Religion* (New York: Harcourt Brace Jovanovich, 1959); Yi Fu Tuan, *Space and Place: The Perspective of Experience* (Minneapolis, MN: The University of Minnesota Press, 1977); Yi Fu Tuan, *Topophilia: A Study of Environmental Perception, Values, and Attitudes* (New York: Columbia University Press, 1990).

CHAPTER THREE

1   Anthony Giddens, *Modernity and Self-Identity: Self and Society in the Late Modern Age* (Stanford, CA: Stanford University Press, 1991). See Norman Vincent Peale, *The Power of Positive Thinking* (New York: Simon and Schuster, 1952); Stephen R. Covey, *The Seven Habits of Highly Effective People* (New York: Free Press, 1989); M. Scott Peck, *The Road Less Travelled: A New Psychology of Love, Traditional Values and Spiritual Growth* (New York: Simon and Schuster, 1978); and Joel Osteen, *Your Best Life Now: 7 Steps to Living at Your Full Potential* (New York: Faithwords, 2004). Eva Illlouz, *Saving the Modern Soul: Therapy, Emotions, and the Culture of Self-Help* (Berkeley: University of California Press, 2008), 9. Reference is to *The Sopranos*. Frank Furedi, *Therapy Culture: Cultivating Vulnerability in an Uncertain Age* (New York: Routledge, 2003), 12.

2   Dr. Phil is Phil McGraw. See, for two examples, Phil McGraw, *Self Matters: Creating Your Life from the Inside Out* (New York: Free Press, 2003); and Phil McGraw, *Real Life: Preparing for the 7 Most Challenging Days of Your Life* (New York: Free Press, 2009).

3   C. Peter Wagner, *The Third Wave of the Holy Spirit: Encountering the Power of Signs and Wonders* (Ann Arbor, MI: Vine Books, 1988), 30–32.

4   Charles H. Kraft, "Response." In *Wrestling with Dark Angels: Toward a Deeper Understanding of the Supernatural Forces in Spiritual Warfare*, edited by C. Peter Wagner and F. Douglas Pennoyer (Ventura, CA: Regal Books, 1990), 274.

5   For example, Eddie Smith suggests that the "Western church has embraced pop-psychology's implication that lack of love, low self-esteem, difficulty paying attention, or any feelings of rejection are abnormal, and they promise that everyone's life can be easily adjusted with enough counseling and medication." Eddie Smith, *Breaking the Enemy's Grip* (Minneapolis, MN: Bethany House Publishers, 2004), 56. Also see Alice Smith, *Beyond the Lie: Finding Freedom from the Past* (Minneapolis, MN: Bethany House Publishers, 2006), 11.

6   Eddie Smith 2004, 17, 88. Rebecca Greenwood, *Let Our Children Go: Steps to Free Your Child from Evil Influences and Demonic Harassment* (Lake Mary, FL: Charisma House, 2011), 95, 146.

7   Alice Smith 2006, 132–133. Kevin Lewis O'Neill, *City of God: Christian Citizenship in Postwar Guatemala* (Berkeley: University of California Press, 2010), 83.

8   See Paul Eli Ivey, "Harmonialism and Metaphysical Religion," in *Encyclopedia of Religion in America*, ed. Charles H. Lippy and Peter W. Williams (Washington, DC: CQ Press, 2010); Stephen Gottschalk, *The Emergence of Christian Science in American Religious Life* (Berkeley: University of California Press, 1979); Beryl Satter, *Each Mind a Kingdom: American Women, Sexual Purity, and the New Thought Movement, 1875–1920* (Berkeley: University of California Press, 2001);

Jill Watts, *God, Harlem USA: The Father Divine Story* (Berkeley: University of California Press, 1995); Carol V. R. George, *God's Salesman: Norman Vincent Peale and the Power of Positive Thinking* (New York: Oxford University Press, 1993); Dennis Voskuil, *Mountains into Goldmines: Robert Schuller and the Gospel of Success* (Grand Rapids, MI: Eerdmans, 1983); Michael Brown, *The Channeling Zone: American Spirituality in an Age of Anxiety* (Cambridge, MA: Harvard University Press, 1997); "Ramtha's School of Enlightenment." www. Ramtha.com (accessed August 30, 2012); and Milmon Harrison, *Righteous Riches: The Word of Faith Movement in Contemporary African American Religion* (New York: Oxford University Press, 2005).

9   Rhonda Byrne, *The Secret* (New York: Atria Books, 2006). Jane Lampman, "'The Secret,' a Phenomenon, is no mystery to many," *The Christian Science Monitor,* March 28, 2007, www.csmonitor.com/2007/0328/p13s01-lire.html (accessed August 30, 2013).

10   Greenwood 2011, 132, 139, 145.

11   Alice Smith 2006, 113, 39.

12   Illouz 2008, 173.

13   For a list, see Rebecca Greenwood, *Breaking the Bonds of Evil: How to Set People Free from Demonic Oppression* (Grand Rapids, MI: Chosen, 2006), 90–91.

14   Alice Smith 2006, 13, ff.

15   Greenwood 2006, 91–92, 108. Greenwood 2011, 100–101.

16   Illouz 2008, 182.

17   Alice Smith, 2006, 19. Eddie Smith 2004, 67, 72.

18   Illouz 2008, 177. Also see Alon Nahi and Haim Omer, "Demonic and Tragic Narratives in Psychotherapy," inn *Healing Plots: The Narrative Basis of Psychotherapy*, ed. Amia Lieblich, Dan McAdams, and Ruthellen Josselson. (Washington, DC: American Psychological Association, 2004), 29–48.

19   Alice Smith 2006, 39.

20   See Edward Ingebretson, SJ, *Maps of Heaven, Maps of Hell: Religious Terror as Memory from the Puritans to Stephen King* (London: M.E. Sharpe, 1996); and Jason Bivins, *Religion of Fear: The Politics of Horror in Conservative Evangelicalism* (New York: Oxford University Press, 2008).

21   Jeffrey Andrew Weinstock, "Introduction: The Spectral Turn," in *Spectral America: Phantoms and the National Imagination*, ed. Jeffrey Andrew Weinstock. (Madison: The University of Wisconsin Press, 2004), 3.

22   See the 2007 Pew "U.S. Religious Landscape Survey," which suggested that 68 percent of Americans believe in angels and demons; http://pewresearch.org/databank/dailynumber/?NumberID=885. Accessed March 1, 2013. Pew Research Center, "Many Americans Mix Multiple Faiths." (np: December 2009), 2; Gallup, "One-Third of Americans Believe Dearly May not Have Departed," http://www.gallup.com/poll/17275/onethird-americans-believe-dearly-may-departed.aspx.

(Accessed 4/9/10); and CBS News, "Poll: Majority Believe in Ghosts," www.cbsnews.com/stories/2005/10/29/opinion/polls/main994766.shtml (accessed September 9, 2013).

23 Robert Wuthnow, *After Heaven: Spirituality in America Since the 1950s* (Berkeley: University of California Press, 1998), 123. Julian Holloway and James Kneale, "Locating Haunting: A Ghost-Hunter's Guide," *Cultural Geographies* 15, no. 3 (2008): 298.

24 Susan Kwilecki, "Twenty-First-Century American Ghosts: The After-Death Communication-Therapy and Revelation from Beyond the Grave," *Religion and American Culture* 19, no. 1 (2009): 23, 24.

25 Michael Cuneo, *American Exorcism: Expelling Demons in the Land of Plenty* (New York: Broadway Books, 2001), xv.

26 Janice Peck, "Psychologized Religion in a Mediated World," in *Rethinking Media, Religion, and Culture*, ed. Stewart M. Hoover and Knut Lundby (Thousand Oaks, CA: Sage Publications, 1997), 234. Also see Janice Peck, *The Age of Oprah: Cultural Icon for the Neoliberal Era* (Boulder, CO: Paradigm Publishers, 2008).

27 The social theorist Anthony Giddens writes that "in conditions of high modernity, we all not only follow lifestyles, but in an important sense are forced to do so—we have no choice but to choose." See Anthony Giddens, *Modernity and Self-Identity: Self and Society in the Late Modern Age* (Stanford, CA: Stanford University Press, 1991), 81. With regards to the influence of consumer capitalism, he writes that "modernity opens up the project of the self, but under conditions strongly influenced by standardizing effects of commodity capitalism." Ibid., 196.

28 Avery Gordon, *Ghostly Matters: Haunting and the Sociological Imagination* (Minneapolis: University of Minnesota Press, 2008), xvi.

29 Judith Richardson, *Possessions: The History and Uses of Haunting in the Hudson Valley* (Cambridge, MA: Harvard University Press, 2003), 3, 119.

30 Chuck D. Pierce and Rebecca Wagner Systema, *Protecting Your Home From Spiritual Darkness* (Ventura, CA: Regal Books, 2004), 61, 42.

31 Pierce and Systema 2004, 42, 61–62.

32 Ed Murphy, *The Handbook of Spiritual Warfare*, revised and updated (Nashville, TN: Thomas Nelson Publishers, 2003), 118.

33 Murphy 2003, 118.

34 I use "phantasmagoric" here not in its sense of the optical illusion created by a magic lantern, but rather its meaning as an unnatural/supernatural conjuration of an apparition. In using the term, I also reference Marina Warner's suggestion that "modernity did not by any means put an end to the quest for spirit and the desire to explain its mystery; curiosity about spirits of every sort (to use Oberon's phrase) and the ideas and imagery which communicate their nature have flourished more vigorously than ever since the seventeenth

century, when the modern fusion of scientific inquiry, psychology, and meta-physics began." Marina Warner, *Phantasmagoria: Spirit Visions, Metaphors, and Media into the Twenty-first Century* (New York: Oxford University Press, 2006), 10.

35 Pierce and Systena 2004, 21.

36 F. Douglas Pennoyer, "In Dark Dungeons of Collective Captivity," in *Wrestling with Dark Angels: Toward a Deeper Understanding of the Supernatural Forces in Spiritual Warfare*, ed. C. Peter Wagner and F. Douglas Pennoyer (Ventura, CA: Regal Books, 1990), 250. Ed Murphy, "We are at War," in *Wrestling with Dark Angels*, 264–265.

37 For most scholars, a dramatic, "born again" conversion experience is one of the defining factors of evangelicalism. See, for example, Michael Emerson and Christian Smith, *Divided by Faith: Evangelical Religion and the Problem of Race in America* (New York: Oxford University Press, 2000), 3. More broadly, the American religious historian R. Marie Griffith has argued that the concep-tion of a "new birth" moves beyond evangelicalism to become a trope used by multiple American religious groups who have correlated transformed (and purified) physical bodies with the state of one's soul. R. Marie Griffith, *Born Again Bodies: Flesh and Spirit in American Christianity* (Berkeley: University of California Press, 2004).

38 Grant Wacker, "Pentecostalism," in *The Encyclopedia of the American Reli-gious Experience*, ed. Charles Lippy and Peter Williams (New York: Scribners, 1988), 933–945.

39 Frank and Ida Mae Hammond, *Pigs in the Parlor: The Practical Guide to De-liverance* (Kirkwood, MO: Impact Christian Books, 2008), 11.

40 Murphy 2003, 60.

41 Murphy 1990, 65. Murphy 2003, 439, 440.

42 Murphy 1990, 68. He lists four "primary sin areas," the other three being "deep-seated anger, bitterness, hatred, rage and rebellion." "a sense of rejection, guilt, poor self-esteem, unworthiness and shame," and "strange attraction to the occult and to the spirit world."

43 Eddie and Alice Smith, *Spiritual Housecleaning Workbook: Amazing Stories and Practical Steps on How to Protect Your Home and Family from Spiritual Pollution* (Ventura, CA: Regal Books, 2007), 71–72.

44 I am struck by how the Third Wave language of an "invitation" to demonic oppression mirrors vampire tales that suggest the creature cannot pass through an entrance or over a threshold unless it is explicitly invited to enter by the human on the other side. See for example, Bram Stoker, *Dracula*. Norton Criti-cal Edition, ed. Nina Auerbach and David J. Skal (New York: W. W. Norton & Company, 1996). Also see Toma Alfredson, director, *Lat den ratte komma in* (*Let the Right One In*) (Magnolia, 2008).

45 Pierce and Systema 2004, 62.

46 Anthony Giddens, *Modernity and Self-Identity: Self and Society in the Late Modern Age* (Stanford, CA: Stanford University Press, 1991).

47 Murphy 2003, 437; Pierce and Systema 2004, 63.

48 Pierce and Systema 2004, 63, 64. Murphy 2003, 439. The four items come from Cindy Jacobs, *The Voice of God: How God Speaks Personally and Corporately to His Children Today* (Ventura, CA: Regal Books, 1995), 65–67.

49 Murphy 2003, 437, 438.

50 Murphy 2003, 472, 473. For an examination of the numerous satanic ritual abuse claims and satanic cult panics of the 1980s and early 1990s, see David Frankfurter, *Evil Incarnate: Rumors of Demonic Conspiracy and Satanic Abuse in History* (Princeton, NJ: Princeton University Press, 2006); and Jeffrey Victor, *Satanic Panic: The Creation of a Contemporary Legend* (Chicago: Open Court Press, 1993).

51 Pierce and Systema 2004, 10.

52 Though not the focus of this chapter, one could suggest several ways in which the Third Wave's theology of demon deliverance has some correspondences to contemporary literatures of addiction—even though spiritual warfare manuals do not make such connections. These include the parallels of generational inheritance, the conception of addiction/demonic oppression as a lifetime struggle, and the complex role of constraint and agency (choice and imposition) in understanding the addict's/demonically afflicted's actions. For an examination of addiction, see Gabor Mate, in *the Realm of Hungry Ghosts: Close Encounters with Addiction* (Berkeley, CA: North Atlantic Books, 2010).

53 For an author discussing demonization as a gradual process, see Cindy Jacobs, *Deliver Us from Evil: Putting a Stop to the Occultic Influence Invading your Home and Community* (Ventura, CA: Regal Books, 2001), 193. Pierce and Systema 2004, 74. Greenwood 2006, 177. Murphy 2003, 476, 109. For the story of John the Satanist, see Greenwood 2006, 178–179. For the story of Audrey, who fasted herself to death due to demonization, see Murphy 2003, 446–448.

54 Pierce and Systema 2004, 37.

55 Eddie and Alice Smith 2007, 58.

56 Murphy 2003, 593.

57 Bill Ellis, *Raising the Devil: Satanism, New Religions, and the Media* (Lexington: The University Press of Kentucky, 2000), 12.

58 Frank and Ida Mae Hammond 1973, 123.

59 Murphy 2003, 593, 594.

60 Frank and Ida Mae Hammond 1973, 22. Jacobs 1994, 106, 108. Murphy 2003, 36.

61 Pierce and Systema 2004, 54, 100–101. Frank and Ida Mae Hammond 1973, 82–83.

62 In Ida Mae Hammond's deliverance of the six-year-old girl, for example, the final call for demons to exit resulted in the child throwing up a huge slime ball.

Frank and Ida Mae Hammond 1973, 84. Word of Faith Fellowship in Spindale, NC. See Cuneo 2001, 183–192. Greenwood 2006, 173.

63 Michel de Certeau, *The Possession at Loudun*, transl. Michael B. Smith (Chicago: The University of Chicago Press, 2000), 2.

64 For an insightful study of conservative Protestantism, Christian Right politics, and the demonization of various American popular cultures, see Bivins 2008.

65 Eddie Smith 2004, 52; Greenwood 2006, 159. For Greenwood's citation of Smith that victims are always partly to blame for their own demonization, see Greenwood 2011, 94. For the quotation about the choice of choosing an ungodly lifestyle, see Greenwood 2006, 93.

66 Cuneo 2001, vx.

67 See Catherine Spooner and Emma McEvoy, "Introduction," in *The Routledge Companion to Gothic*, ed. Catherine Spooner and Emma McEvoy (New York: Routledge, 2007). See Sigmund Freud, *The Uncanny* (New York: Penguin Classics, 2003), 148; Murphy 2003, 60, 109; Pierce and Systema 2004, 74. See Mark Edmundsen, *Nightmares on Main Street: Angels, Sadomasochism, and the Culture of Gothic* (Cambridge, MA: Harvard University Press, 1997), xiv.

68 Thomas Csordas, *The Sacred Self: A Cultural Phenomenology of Charismatic Healing* (Berkeley: University of California Press, 1994), 165.

69 As an aside, one might ask, what is the "force" referred to in the phrase "force of habit?" In particular, what is the force of habit involved with those ideas and practices often identified as "religious"? While individual psychological elements are at play, the force is first and foremost social. It is the social habituation inculcated into our bodies, thinking, and acting. The religious gesture enacted during stress, the repeated phrase uttered in response to an event, the violent outburst shouted when feeling betrayed—these are the immediately available tools of reaction, the most accessible without forethought, the quickest performance in one's repertoire of possibilities. These are responses from the force of habit.

In discussing the demons of spiritual warfare—or the statistical reliability of social reproduction—force of habit is the tendency to reproduce the constraints and violences with which social locations have scarred individuals. The reproduction of structures and dispositions, as instantiated in our socially habituated subjectivities, is not automatic and inevitable, but it is likely because force of habit makes alternatives less likely, less accessible, less palpable. But forces of habit can be broken. This may occur when those predominant responses don't work, whether because the individual is placed into a new social situation, or when larger social structures themselves break down—when the once established becomes the disestablished. How can people come to perceive that the forces of habit which entrap them are not demons, but mere phantoms? What are the events, disjunctions, gaps, and desires that can unveil the demons as illusory? While this subject is far afield from the focus of this chapter (and my description of it here a bit too precious), it is a crucial question when one seeks to banish the ghosts of the past, however they might be envisioned. For a discussion of the social mapping of this sort of "metanoia" in the work of social theorist Pierre Bourdieu, see Sean McCloud, "The Possibilities of Change in a World of Constraint: Individual and Social Transformation in the Work of Pierre Bourdieu," *Bulletin for the Study of Religion* 41, no. 1 (2012): 2–8.

70 Csordas 1994, 180, 187.

71 Csordas 1994, 43.

72 For one example see the American film *Ghost* and then, for contrast, watch the Japanese film *Ju-On*.

CHAPTER FOUR

1 Alice Smith, *Beyond the Lie: Finding Freedom from the Past* (Minneapolis, MN: Bethany House Publishers, 2006), 139.

2 Cindy Jacobs, *Possessing the Gates of the Enemy: A Training Manual for Militant Intercession*, second Edition with study guide (Grand Rapids, MI: Baker Books, 1994), 141.

3 Rebecca Greenwood, *Breaking the Bonds of Evil: How to Set People Free from Demonic Oppression* (Grand Rapids, MI: Chosen, 2006), 126, 127.

4 Jacobs 1994, 142.

5 Greenwood 2006, 127.

6 Jacobs 1994, 142.

7 Ed Murphy, *The Handbook for Spiritual Warfare*, revised and updated (Nashville: Thomas Nelson Publishers, 2003), 442, 433. Greenwood 2006, 149.

8 Jacobs 1994, 132–133, 142–143. Greenwood 2006, 164–165.

9 Jacobs 1994, 166. Rebecca Greenwood, *Let Our Children Go: Steps to Free Your Child from Evil Influences and Demonic Harassment* (Lake Mary, FL: Charisma House, 2011), 32. Greenwood 2006, 127, 139–143, 79.

10 Murphy 2003, 146, 153.

11 Greenwood 2011, 90, 114.

12 Murphy 2003, 135.

13 Jacobs 1994, 48, 26–27. Greenwood 2006, 129.

14 Jacobs 1994, 93. Harold Caballeros, *Victorious Warfare: Discovering Your Rightful Place in God's Kingdom* (Nashville, TN: Thomas Nelson Publishers, 2001), xii. C. Peter Wagner, *Warfare Prayer: How to Seek God's Power and Protection in the Battle to Build His Kingdom* (Ventura, CA: Regal Books, 1992), 54.

15 Caballeros 2001, xii. Caballeros, his large church, and their intercessory activities are described in detail in Kevin Lewis O'Neill, *City of God: Christian Citizenship in Postwar Guatemala* (Berkeley: University of California Press,

2010). O'Neill's assessment of Guatemalan neo-Pentecostalism is largely applicable to the US context. Jacobs 1994, 52–53, 92, 154, 48–49, 97–98, 150, 67.

[16] Greenwood 2011, 71, 67.

[17] Jacobs 1994, 147. Murphy 2003, 444.

[18] Max Weber, "The Social Psychology of the World's Religions," in *From Max Weber: Essays in Sociology*, ed. H. H. Gerth and C. Wright Mills (New York: Oxford University Press, 1946), 280.

[19] Alice Smith 2006, 71.

[20] Caballeros 2001, 119. While Caballeros' view on the power of demonic structures is widely shared, there are some Third Wave well-wishers who disagree. For instance, in 1994, Charles Kraft asserted that "if the structures themselves were under demonic control, there would be no possibility for people to get released from them. The people would be totally determined by the evil system." Instead, Kraft argues that demonic control is always "personal (even when persons are in groups)." See Charles Kraft, "Response," in *Wrestling with Dark Angels: Toward a Deeper Understanding of the Supernatural Forces in Spiritual Warfare*, ed. C. Peter Wagner and F. Douglas Pennoyer (Ventura, CA: Regal Books, 1990), 274–275.

[21] Caballeros 2001, 119.

[22] George Otis Jr., *Informed Intercession* (Ventura: Renew Books, 1999), 141.

[23] Otis Jr., 1999, 201. The full quotation reads, "If we want to argue that the alcoholism plaguing Native peoples in Canada is the legacy of ancient spiritual pacts, we must first examine several viable counter-arguments—including the suggestions that the problem stems from modern social injustice." In a footnote on page 213, he concludes about this situation that, "in this case the truth embraces both explanations."

[24] See, for one of the dozens of media reports on his statement, CNN's "Pat Robertson says Haiti paying for 'pact to the devil,'" January 13, 2010, www.cnn.com/2010/US/01/13/haiti.pat.robertson/index.html. Accessed 5 June 2013.

[25] Greenwood 2006, 23. Murphy 2003, 52, 53.

[26] Greenwood 2006, 25. Murphy 2003, 54.

[27] Greenwood 2006, 63; Alice Smith 2006, 80.118.

[28] See, for example, Ann Swidler, *Talk of Love: How Culture Matters* (Chicago: The University of Chicago Press, 2001).

[29] Sean McCloud, *Divine Hierarchies: Class in American Religion and Religious Studies* (Chapel Hill: The University of North Carolina Press, 2007), 112–118.

[30] See Milton Friedman, *Capitalism and Freedom* (Chicago: The University of Chicago Press, 1962), and Milton Freedman, *Free to Choose* (New York: Harcourt Brace Jovanovich, 1980). In suggesting that neoliberalism has historical precedents, it is accurate to note that the conception of the freely willed and autonomous individual that I focus on here is a liberal concept one can trace back to writers such as John Locke.

31 Pierre Bourdieu, "The Essence of Neoliberalism," *Le Monde diplomatique,* English edition (December 1998), http://mondediplo.com/1998/12/08bourdieu/. Accessed July 20, 2012.

32 See Simon Clarke, "The Neoliberal Theory of Society," in *Neoliberalism: A Critical Reader,* ed. Alfredo Saad-Filho and Deborah Johnston (London: Pluto Press, 2005), 51; and Daniel T. Rodgers, *Age of Fracture* (Cambridge, MA: Belknap/Harvard University Press, 2011), 219.

33 Bethany Moreton, *To Serve God and Wal-Mart: The Making of Christian Free Enterprise* (Cambridge, MA: Harvard University Press, 2009), 126.

34 Roy—who does not use the term "neoliberalism"—sees the divorce between religions and their environing cultures to be more expansive and widespread in the contemporary period. He argues that "secularization and globalization have forced religions to break away from culture" and suggests that "in order to circulate, the religious object must appear universal, disconnected from a specific culture that has to be understood in order for the message to be grasped. Religion therefore circulates outside knowledge. Salvation does not require people to know, but to believe." See Olivier Roy, *Holy Ignorance: When Religion and Culture Part Ways* (New York: Columbia University Press, 2010), 2, 6. For a volume that specifically discusses religion and neoliberalism with regards to state regulation and religious charity, see Tuomas Martikainen and Francois Gauthier, eds., *Religion in a Neoliberal Age: Political Economy and Modes of Governance* (Burlington, VT: Ashgate, 2013).

35 Jean and John Comaroff, "Millennial Capitalism: First Thoughts on a Second Coming," in *Millennial Capitalism and the Culture of Neoliberalism,* ed. Jean and John Comaroff (Durham, NC: Duke University Press, 2001), 13.

36 Daniel Rodgers, *Age of Fracture* (Cambridge, MA: Belknap/Harvard University Press, 2011), 5, 6.

37 I argue that the work of Pierre Bourdieu offers a useful entrance into mapping the relationships between agency and structure. See Sean McCloud, "The Possibilities of Change in a World of Constraint: Individual and Social Transformation in the Work of Pierre Bourdieu," *Bulletin for the Study of Religion* 41, no. 1 (2012): 2–8.

38 If anything, though, it seems that those who study and write about American religions specifically tend to err on the side of reading too little structural influence (and perhaps too much consciousness) into the activities of their subjects. I agree with Kathryn Lofton when she writes that "I have become increasingly concerned that in our scholarly ambition to translate our subjects—to, as the phrasing often goes, take our subjects seriously—we have become sycophants to our subjects, reframing every act as an inevitably creative act." See Kathryn Lofton, *Oprah: The Gospel of an Icon* (Berkeley: University of California Press, 2011), 16. As scholars of American religion, we corporately need to think more—and more deeply—about conceptions of "agency," "structure," and "consciousness."

39 For a cultural history of reverb, see Peter Doyle, *Echo and Reverb: Fabricating Space in Popular Music Recording, 1900–1960* (Middletown, CT: Wesleyan University Press, 2005). For considerations of the kinds of cultural work that reverberation and noise can do, see Benjamin Halligan, Paul Hegarty, and Michael Goddard, eds., *Reverberations: The Philosophy, Aesthetics and Politics of Noise* (New York: Continuum, 2012). In terms of scholarship on American religion, little attention has been given to the topic of "sound." For two notable exceptions, see Isaac Weiner, "Sound and American Religions," *Religion Compass* 3, no. 5 (2009): 897–908, and Leigh Schmidt, *Hearing Things: Religion, Illusion, and the American Enlightenment* (Cambridge, MA: Harvard University Press, 2000). Much more work has been done on American religion and popular-music styles. See, for just two examples focused on contemporary evangelicalism, Eileen Luhr, *Witnessing Suburbia: Conservatives and Christian Youth Culture* (Berkeley: University of California Press, 2009), and David W. Stowe, *No Sympathy for the Devil: Christian Pop Music and the Transformation of American Evangelicalism* (Chapel Hill: The University of North Carolina Press, 2011). These studies of sound and music are textual, of course, and not aural. Jason Bivins recently asked in his essay on the *frequencies* 100 essays series, "what would happen if, instead of looking to a different kind of writing that would provide release for the author and diversion for the reader, we thought seriously about the vibratory, circulatory dimensions of this project and dove headlong into the possibilities of this format. Perhaps a second 100 might avoid words altogether. Let there be sculpture, sound, and dance. Let there be video, collage, and cooking." See Jason Bivins, "Get It On," *frequencies* (April 10, 2012), http://blogs.ssrc.org/tif/2012/04/10/get-it-on/. Accessed July 21, 2012.

40 One might imagine here the drop-tuned sounds of contemporary drone metal bands such as Monarch! or Moss. One might also think of Mares of Thrace, whose guitarist/composer G. Therese Lanz uses a baritone guitar to achieve low tones.

41 Bethany Moreton, "The Soul of Neoliberalism," *Social Text* 92 25:3 (Fall 2007): 117.

42 See Birgit Meyer, "Pentecostalism and Neo-Liberal Capitalism: Faith, Prosperity and Vision in African Pentecostal-Charismatic Churches," *Journal for the Study of Religion* 20, no. 2 (2007): 5–28; Kevin Lewis O'Neill, *City of God: Christian Citizenship in Postwar Guatemala* (Berkeley: University of California Press, 2010), and David Martin, *Pentecostalism: The World Their Parish* (Boston: Wiley-Blackwell, 2001).

43 Meyer, 21.

44 See Edward Silvoso, *Anointed for Business: How to Use Your Influence in the Marketplace to Change the World* (Ventura, CA: Regal Books, 2002), and

Transformation: Change the Marketplace and You Change the World (Ventura, CA: Regal Books, 2010).

45 Alice Patterson, *Bridging the Racial and Political Divide: How Godly Politics Can Transform a Nation* (San Jose, CA: Transformational Publications—A Division of Harvest Evangelism, 2010), 186.

46 Cindy Jacobs, *The Reformation Manifesto* (Minneapolis, MN: Bethany House Publishers, 2008), 164.

47 Patterson 2010, 186–189.

48 Jacobs 2001, 212.

49 Jacobs 1994, 143.

50 There are many published versions of Conwell's speech. For an Internet version, see www.americanrhetoric.com/speeches/rconwellacresofdiamonds.htm. Accessed June 10, 2013.

51 Tom Rose, *Economics: Principles and Policies from a Christian Perspective* (Mercer, PA: American Enterprise Publications, 1986).

52 Jacobs 2008, 161–162, 165, 166. Despite the fact that John Maynard Keynes was an agnostic, member of the Liberal Party, anticommunist, and anti-Marxist, Jacobs incorrectly identifies him as "an atheist and a Fabian socialist who believed all the world's problems would one day be solved by a global, socialist government." Jacobs 2008, endnote 10 on page 227.

53 Jacobs 2008, 171, 166, 168, 175.

54 For a recent study of human rights discourse and neoliberalism in Argentina, see Karen Faulk, *In the Wake of Neoliberalism: Citizenship and Human Rights in Argentina* (Standford, CA: Stanford University Press, 2012).

55 Greenwood 2006, 26, 96, 21; Alice Smith 2006, 70; Eddie Smith 2004, 48. Rebecca Greenwood, *Authority to Tread: An Intercessor's Guide to Strategic-Level Spiritual Warfare* (Grand Rapids, MI: Chosen, 2005), 126.

56 Greenwood 2006, 28.

CONCLUSION

1 For the story on Pope Francis, see Anthony Faiola, "A Modern Pope Gets Old School on the Devil," *Washington Post* (May 10, 2014). Accessed June 19, 2014, www.washingtonpost.com/world/a-modern-pope-gets-old-school-on-the-devil/2014/05/10/f56a9354-1b93-4662-abbb-d877e49f15ea_story.html. Jennifer Percy, *Demon Camp: A Soldier's Exorcism* (New York: Scribner's, 2014); "Fighting Satan" aired on the Oprah Network's *Our America with Lisa Ling* on May 29, 2014; Katie Jagel, "Poll Results: Exorcism," *YouGov: What the World Thinks* (September 17, 2013). Accessed June 19, 2014, today.yougov.com/news/2013/09/17/poll-results-exorcism/.

For a discussion on the pervasiveness of spiritual warfare and the belief in demons in evangelicalism (and how scholars of religion continue to ignore it), see Andrew Monteith, "Demons, Exoticism, and the Academy," *The Religious Studies Project* (April 17, 2014). Accessed June 19, 2014, www.religiousstudiesproject.com/2014/04/17/demons-exoticism-and-the-academy-by-andrew-monteith/. Monteith's article was spurred by similar statements I made in an interview on my research for this book. See Dave McConeghy, "Demons, Possessions, and Exorcisms: Sean McCloud on Spiritual Warfare," *Religious Studies Project* (April 14, 2014). Accessed June 19, 2014, www.religiousstudiesproject.com/podcast/sean-mccloud-on-spiritual-warfare/.

2   Jean Comaroff, "The Politics of Conviction: Faith on the Neoliberal Frontier," in *Contemporary Religiosities: Emergent Socialities and the Post-Nation-State*, ed. Bruce Kapferer, Kari Telle, and Annelin Eriksen (New York: Berghahn Books, 2010), 17.

3   Otis Jr. 1999, 79. Otis, Jr., George. *Informed Intercession*. Ventura: Renew Books, 1999.

4   C. Peter Wagner, "The Visible and the Invisible," in *Breaking Strongholds in Your City: How to Use Spiritual Mapping to Make Your Prayers More Strategic, Effective and Targeted*, ed. C. Peter Wagner (Ventura, CA: Regal Books, 1993), 49.

5   Wagner, "The Visible and the Invisible" 1993, 49.

6   Wagner, "The Visible and the Invisible" 1993, 49.

7   For excellent examples of the promotion of prayer over social action and the individualization of social problems among Harold Caballeros' Guatemalan congregants, see O' Neill 2010. O' Neill, Kevin Lewis. *City of God: Christian Citizenship in Postwar Guatemala*. Berkeley: University of California Press, 2010.

8   Comaroff 2010, 30.

9   Matthew Wood, "Capital Possession: A Comparative Approach to 'New Age' Control of the Means of Possession," *Culture and Religion* 4, no. 1 (2003): 177.

10 In arguing this, I heed the caveats lodged by Todd Sanders concerning what he sees as conventional anthropological analysis of occult entities and activities as third world critiques of neoliberal infiltrations. See Todd Sanders, "Buses in Bongoland: Seductive Analytics and the Occult," *Anthropological Theory* 8, no. 2 (2008): 107–132. The demons of Third Wave spiritual warfare are not simply critiques of late-modern neoliberalism, but rather express ambivalence with the social formation.

BIBLIOGRAPHY

Albanese, Catherine. "The Culture of Religious Combining: Reflections for the New American Millennium." *Crosscurrents* (Spring/Summer 2000): 16–22.

Alfano, Sean. "Poll: The Majority Believe in Ghosts." *CBS News Online* (February 11, 2009). http://www.cbsnews.com/stories/2005/10/29/opinion/polls/main994766.shtml. Accessed August 4, 2012.

Alfredson, Toma (director). *Lat den ratte komma in* (*Let the Right One In*). Magnolia, 2008.

Allison, Greg. *Historical Theology: An Introduction to Christian Doctrine*. Grand Rapids, MI: Zondervan, 2011.

Bader, Christopher D., Mencken, F. Carson, and Joseph O. Baker. *Paranormal America: Ghost Encounters, UFO Sightings, Bigfoot Hunts, and Other Curiosities in Religion and Culture*. New York: New York University Press, 2010.

Baker, Kelly. *Gospel According to the Klan: The KKK's Appeal to Protestant America, 1915–1930*. Lawrence: University Press of Kansas, 2011.

Balmer, Randall. *Encyclopedia of Evangelicalism*. Louisville, KY: WJK Press, 2002.

Barkun, Michael. *A Culture of Conspiracy: Apocalyptic Visions in Contemporary America*. Berkeley: University of California Press, 2006.

Beckett, Bob. "Practical Steps Toward Community Deliverance." In *Breaking Strongholds in Your City: How to use Spiritual Mapping to Make Your Prayers More Strategic, Effective and Targeted*. Edited by C. Peter Wagner. Ventura, CA: Regal Books, 1993, 147–170.

Beilby, James K. and Paul Rhodes Eddy, eds.. *Understanding Spiritual Warfare: Four Views*. Grand Rapids, MI: Baker Academic, 2012.

Bender, Courtney. *The New Metaphysicals: Spirituality and the American Religious Imagination*. Chicago: The University of Chicago Press, 2010.

——— and Pamela Klassen, eds. *After Pluralism: Reimagining Religious Engagement*. New York: Columbia University Press, 2010.

Berger, Helen and Douglas Ezzy. *Teenage Witches: Magical Youth and the Search for the Self*. New Brunswick, NJ: Rutgers University Press, 2007.

Bergland, Renee L. *The National Uncanny: Indian Ghosts and American Subjects*. Hanover, NH: Dartmouth College Press, 2000.

Berkhofer Jr., Robert F. *The White Man's Indian: Images of the American Indian from Columbus to the Present*. New York: Vintage Books, 1978.

Berlitz, Charles. *The Bermuda Triangle*. New York: Doubleday, 1974.

Biles, Jeremy, "Out of this World: The Materiality of the Beyond." In *Religion and Material Culture: The Matter of Belief*. Edited by David Morgan, 135–152. New York: Routledge, 2010.

Bivins, Jason. *Religion of Fear: The Politics of Horror in Conservative Evangelicalism*. New York: Oxford University Press, 2008.

———. "Get It On." *frequencies* (April 10, 2012). http://blogs.ssrc.org/tif/2012/04/10/get-it-on/. Accessed July 21, 2012.

———. "'Only One Repertory:' American Religious Studies." *Religion* 42, no. 3 (2012): 395–407.

Blum, Edward J. and Paul Harvey. *The Color of Christ: The Son of God and the Saga of Race in America*. Chapel Hill: The University of North Carolina Press, 2012.

Boivin, Nicole. "Grasping the Elusive and Unknowable: Material Culture in Ritual Practice." *Material Religion* 5, no. 3 (2009): 266–287.

Bourdieu, Pierre. "The Essence of Neoliberalism." *Le Monde diplomatique*. English Edition. December 1998. http://mondediplo.com/1998/12/08bourdieu/. Accessed July 20, 2012.

Brakke, David. *Demons and the Making of the Monk: Spiritual Combat in Early Christianity*. Cambridge, MA: Harvard University Press, 2006.

Braude, Ann. *Radical Spirits: Spiritualism and Women's Rights in Nineteenth-Century America*. Boston: Beacon Press, 1989.

Brown, Michael. *The Channeling Zone: American Spirituality in an Age of Anxiety*. Cambridge, MA: Harvard University Press, 1997.

Bruce, Steve. *God Is Dead: Secularization in the West*. Malden, MA: Wiley-Blackwell, 2002.

Brunvand, Jan. *The Vanishing Hitchhiker: American Urban Legends and their Meanings*. New York: W.W. Norton and Company, 1981.

Buell, Ryan and Stefan Petrucha. *Paranormal State: My Journey into the Unknown*. New York: HarperCollins Publishers, 2010.

Butler, Jon. *Awash in a Sea of Faith: Christianizing the American People*. Cambridge, MA: Harvard University Press, 1992.

Byrne, Rhonda. *The Secret*. New York: Atria Books, 2006.

Caballeros, Harold. "Defeating the Enemy with the Help of Spiritual Mapping." In *Breaking Strongholds in Your City: How to Use Spiritual Mapping to Make Your Prayers More Strategic, Effective and Targeted*. Edited by C. Peter Wagner, 123–146. Ventura, CA: Regal Books, 1993.

———. *Victorious Warfare: Discovering Your Rightful Place in God's Kingdom*. Nashville, TN: Thomas Nelson Publishers, 2001.

Cameron, Ellie. Indigenous Spectrality and the Politics of Postcolonial Ghost Stories. *Cultural Geographies* 15, no. 3 (2008): 383–393.

Campbell, Colin. "Romanticism and the Consumer Ethic: Intimations of a Weber-style Thesis." *Sociological Analysis* 44, no. 4 (1983): 279–295.

Carrette, Jeremy and Richard King, *Selling Spirituality: The Silent Takeover of Religion*. New York: Routledge, 2005.

CBS News. "Poll: Majority Believe in Ghosts." http://www.cbsnews.com/stories/2005/10/29/opinion/polls/main994766.shtml. Accessed September 12, 2012.

Chaves, Mark. *American Religion: Contemporary Trends*. Princeton, NJ: Princeton University Press, 2011.

Chestnut, Andrew. *Devoted to Death: Santa Muerte, the Skeleton Saint*. New York: Oxford University Press, 2012.

Christian Life Editors. *Signs and Wonders Today*. Wheaton, IL: Christian Life Magazine, 1983.

Cimino, Richard and Don Lattin. *Shopping for Faith: American Religion in the New Millennium*. San Francisco, CA: Jossey-Bass, 1998.

Clark, Lynn Schofield. *From Angels to Aliens: Teenagers, the Media, and the Supernatural*. New York: Oxford University Press, 2003.

Clarke, Simon. "The Neoliberal Theory of Society." In Alfredo Saad-Filho and Deborah Johnston, eds., 50–59. *Neoliberalism: A Critical Reader*. London: Pluto Press, 2005.

Coffey, Chip. *Growing up Psychic*. New York: Three Rivers Press, 2012.

Cohen, Lizabeth. *A Consumer's Republic: The Politics of Mass Consumption in Postwar America*. New York: Vintage Books, 2003.

Cohen, Charles L. and Ronald L. Numbers, eds. *Gods in America: Religious Pluralism in the United States*. New York: Oxford University Press, 2013.

Comaroff, Jean. "Uncool Passion: Nietzsche Meets the Pentecostals." Max Weber Lecture No. 2008/10. San Domenico di Fiesole, Italy: European University Institute, 2008.

———. "The Politics of Conviction: Faith on the Neoliberal Frontier." In *Contemporary Religiosities: Emergent Socialities and the Post-Nation-State*, edited by Bruce Kapferer, Kari Telle, and Annelin Eriksen, 17–38. New York: Berghahn Books, 2010.

——— and John L. Comaroff, eds.. *Millennial Capitalism and the Culture of Neoliberalism*. Durham, NC: Duke University Press, 2001.

——— and John Comaroff. "Millennial Capitalism: First Thoughts on a Second Coming." In *Millennial Capitalism and the Culture of Neoliberalism*, edited by Jean and John Comaroff, 1–56. Durham, NC: Duke University Press, 2001.

Connolly, William E. "The Evangelical-Capitalist Resonance Machine." *Political Theory* 33, no. 6 (2005): 869–886.

———. *Capitalism and Christianity, American Style*. Durham, NC: Duke University Press, 2008.

Corrigan, John and Lynn S. Neal, eds. *Religious Intolerance in America: A Documentary History*. Chapel Hill: The University of North Carolina Press, 2010.

Covey, Stephen R. *The Seven Habits of Highly Effective People*. New York: Free Press, 1989.

Cox, Harvey. *Fire from Heaven: The Rise of Pentecostal Spirituality and the Reshaping of Religion in the Twenty-First Century*. Reading, MA: Addison-Wesley, 1995.

Cresswell, Timothy. *Place: A Short Introduction*. Malden, MA: Blackwell, 2004.

Csordas, Thomas. *The Sacred Self: A Cultural Phenomenology of Charismatic Healing*. Berkeley: University of California Press, 1997.

Cuneo, Michael W. *American Exorcism: Expelling Demons in the Land of Plenty*. New York: Broadway Books, 2001.

Curtis, Heather D. "A Sane Gospel: Radical Evangelicals, Psychology, and Pentecostal Revival in the Early Twentieth Century." *Religion and American Culture* 21, no. 2 (2011): 195–226.

Davies, Owen. *Grimoires: A History of Magic Books*. New York: Oxford University Press, 2009.

Davis, David Brion. "Some Themes of Countersubversion: An Analysis of Anti-Masonic, Anti-Catholic, and Anti-Mormon Literature." *The Mississippi Valley Historical Review* 47, no. 2 (September 1960): 205–224.

Dean, Jodi. *Aliens in America: Conspiracy Cultures from Outerspace to Cyberspace*. Ithaca, NY: Cornell University Press, 1998.

DeBernardi, Jean. "Spiritual Warfare and Territorial Spirits: The Globalization and Localization of a 'Practical Theology.'" *Religious Studies and Theology* 18, no. 2 (1999): 66–96.

De Certeau, Michel. *The Possession at Loudon*. Translated by Michael B. Smith. Chicago: The University of Chicago Press, 2000.

DeRogatis, Amy. "'Born Again is a Sexual Term:' Demons, STDs, and God's Healing Sperm." *Journal of the American Academy of Religion* 77, no. 2 (2009): 275–302.

Dochuk, Darren. *From Bible Belt to Sun Belt: Plain-Folk Religion, Grassroots Politics, and the Rise of Evangelical Conservatism*. New York: W. W. Norton and Company, 2011.

Dowland, Seth. "'Family' Values and the Formation of a Christian Right Agenda." *Church History* 78, no. 3 (September 2009): 606–631.

Doyle, Peter. *Echo and Reverb: Fabricating Space in Popular Music Recording, 1900–1960*. Middletown, CT: Wesleyan University Press, 2005.

Duggan, Lisa. *Twilight of Equality? Neoliberalism, Cultural Politics, and the Attack on Democracy*. Boston: Beacon Press, 2003.

Dunn, Richard S., ed.. *The Laws and Liberties of Massachusetts: Reprinted from the Unique Copy of the 1648 Edition in the Henry E.*

Huntington Library. Cambridge, MA: Huntington Library Press, 1998.

Eck, Diana. *A New Religious America: How a "Christian Country" Has Become the World's Most Religiously Diverse Nation*. San Francisco: HarperSanFrancisco, 2002.

Edensor, Tim. "Mundane Hauntings: Commuting through the Phantasmagoric Working-Class Spaces of Manchester, England." *Cultural Geographies* 15, no. 3 (2008): 313–333.

Edmundsen, Mark. *Nightmares on Main Street: Angels, Sadomasochism, and the Culture of Gothic*. Cambridge, MA: Harvard University Press, 1997.

Einstein, Mara. *Brands of Faith: Marketing Religion in a Commercial Age*. New York: Routledge, 2008.

Eliade, Mircea. *The Sacred and the Profane: The Nature of Religion*. New York: Harcourt Brace Jovanovich, 1959.

Ellis, Bill. *Raising the Devil: Satanism, New Religions, and the Media*. Lexington: University Press of Kentucky, 2000.

———. *Lucifer Ascending: The Occult in Folklore and Popular Culture*. Lexington: University Press of Kentucky, 2004.

Emerson, Michael O. and Christian Smith. *Divided by Faith: Evangelical Religion and the Problem of Race in America*. New York: Oxford University Press, 2000.

Faiola, Anthony. "A Modern Pope Gets Old School on the Devil." *Washington Post* (May 10, 2014). http://www.washingtonpost.com/world/a-modern-pope-gets-old-school-on-the-devil/2014/05/10/f56a9354-9351b93-4662-abbb-d877e49f15ea_story.html. Accessed June 19, 2014.

Faulk, Karen. *In the Wake of Neoliberalism: Citizenship and Human Rights in Argentina*. Stanford, CA: Stanford University Press, 2012.

Fessenden, Tracy. *Culture and Redemption: Religion, the Secular, and American Literature*. Princeton, NJ: Princeton University Press, 2006.

———. "The Objects of American Religious Studies." *Religion* 42, no. 3 (2012): 373–382.

Fine, Gary Alan. *Manufacturing Tales: Sex, Money, Contemporary Legends*. Knoxville: University of Tennessee Press, 1992.

——— and Patricia A. Turner. *Whispers on the Color Line: Rumor and Race in America*. Berkeley: University of California Press, 2004.

Finucane, R.C. *Ghosts: Appearances of the Dead and Cultural Transformation*. Amherst, NY: Prometheus, 1996.

Fox, Richard Wightman. *Jesus in America: Personal Savior, Cultural Hero, National Obsession*. San Francisco: HarperOne, 2004.

Franchot, Jenny. *Roads to Rome: The Antebellum Protestant Encounter with Catholicism*. Berkeley: University of California Press, 1994

Frankfurter, David. *Evil Incarnate: Rumors of Demonic Conspiracy and Satanic Abuse in History*. Princeton, NJ: Princeton University Press, 2006.

Freud, Sigmund. *The Uncanny*. New York: Penguin Classics, 2003.

Friedman, Milton. *Capitalism and Freedom*. Chicago: The University of Chicago Press, 1962.

———. *Free to Choose*. New York: Harcourt Brace Jovanovich, 1980.

Furedi, Frank. *Therapy Culture: Cultivating Vulnerability in an Uncertain Age*. New York: Routledge, 2003.

Galbreath, Robert. "Explaining Modern Occultism." In *The Occult in America: New Historical Perspectives*, edited by Howard Kerr and Charles L. Crow, 11–37. Urbana: University of Illinois Press, 1983).

Gauthier, Francois and Tuomas Martikainen, eds.. *Religion in Consumer Society: Brands, Consumers, and Markets*. Burlington, VT: Ashgate, 2013.

Gell, Alfred. *Art and Agency: An Anthropological Theory*. New York: Oxford University Press, 1998.

George, Carol V.R. *God's Salesman: Norman Vincent Peale and the Power of Positive Thinking*. New York: Oxford University Press, 1993.

Gerber, Lynne. *Seeking the Straight and Narrow: Weight Loss and Sexual Reorientation in Evangelical America*. Chicago: The University of Chicago Press, 2012.

Giddens, Anthony. *Modernity and Self-Identity: Self and Society in the Late Modern Age*. Stanford, CA: Stanford University Press, 1991.

Girard, Rene. *Violence and the Sacred*. Translated by Patrick Gregory. Baltimore, MD: The Johns Hopkins University Press, 1979.

Glass, Matthew. "'Alexanders All:' Symbols of Conquest and Resistance at Mount Rushmore." In *American Sacred Space*, edited by David Chidester and Edward Linenthal, 152–186. Bloomington: Indiana University Press, 1995.

Godbeer, Richard. *The Devil's Dominion: Magic and Religion in Early New England*. New York: Cambridge University Press, 1992.

Gordon, Avery. *Ghostly Matters: Haunting and the Sociological Imagination*. Minneapolis: University of Minnesota Press, 1997.

Gottschalk, Stephen. *The Emergence of Christian Science in American Religious Life*. Berkeley: University of California Press, 1979.

Greenhouse, Carol J., ed. *Ethnographies of Neoliberalism*. Philadelphia: University of Pennsylvania Press, 2009

Greenwood, Rebecca. *Authority to Tread: An Intercessor's Guide to Strategic-Level Spiritual Warfare*. Grand Rapids, MI: Chosen, 2005.

Greenwood, Rebecca. *Breaking the Bonds of Evil: How to Set People Free from Demonic Oppression*. Grand Rapids, MI: Chosen, 2006.

———. *Let Our Children Go: Steps to Free Your Child from Evil Influences and Demonic Harassment*. Lake Mary, FL: Charisma House, 2011.

Gregory, Brad. *The Unintended Reformation: How a Religious Revolution Secularized Society*. Cambridge, MA: Belknap/Harvard University Press, 2012.

Griffith, R. Marie. *Born Again Bodies: Flesh and Spirit in American Christianity*. Berkeley: University of California Press, 2004.

Hall, David D. *Worlds of Wonder, Days of Judgment: Popular Religious Belief in Early New England*. Cambridge, MA: Harvard University Press, 1990.

———. (ed). *Witch-Hunting in Seventeenth-Century New England: A Documentary History 1638–1693*. Second Edition. Durham, NC: Duke University Press, 2005.

Halligan, Benjamin; Paul Hegarty; and Michael Goddard, eds. *Reverberations: The Philosophy, Aesthetics and Politics of Noise*. New York: Continuum, 2012.

Hammond, Phillip. *Religion and Personal Autonomy: The Third Disestablishment in America*. Columbia: South Carolina University Press, 1992.

Hammond, Frank and Ida Mae. *Pigs in the Parlor: The Practical Guide to Deliverance*. Kirkwood, MO: Impact Books, 1973.

Hangen, Tona. *Redeeming the Dial: Radio, Religion, and Popular Culture in America*. Chapel Hill: The University of North Carolina Press, 2001.

Harris, Dan, Jackie Jesko, and Jenna Millman. "Teen Girl Exorcism Squad: Three Arizona Girls Claim to Cast Out Demons." *Nightline*, April 5, 2012. http://abcnews.go.com/US/teen-girl-exorcism-squad-arizona-girls-claim-cast/story?id=16074541. Accessed July 13, 2012.

Harrison, Milmon. *Righteous Riches: The Word of Faith Movement in Contemporary African American Religion*. New York: Oxford University Press, 2005.

Harvey, David. *A Brief History of Neoliberalism*. New York: Oxford University Press, 2007.

Heanor, Gwendolyn. "'Fieldworking' Deliverance Rituals in a Liberian Pentecostal Ministry: The Surprising Benefits of Embracing Your 'Otherness' While Taking Part in Religious Performance." *Fieldwork in Religion* 5, no. 2 (2010): 193–206.

Hendershot, Heather. *Shaking the World for Jesus: Media and Conservative Evangelical Culture*. Chicago: University of Chicago Press, 2004.

Hicks, Robert. *In Pursuit of Satan: The Police and the Occult*. Buffalo, NY: Prometheus Books, 1991.

Higham, John. *Strangers in the Land: Patterns of American Nativism, 1860–1925*. New Brunswick, NJ: Rutgers University Press, 2002

Hill, Annette. *Paranormal Media: Audiences, Spirits and Magic in Popular Culture*. New York: Routledge, 2010.

Hofstadter, Richard. *The Paranoid Style in American Politics*. New York: Vintage, 2008.

Holifield, E. Brooks. *A History of Pastoral Care in America: From Salvation to Self-Realization*. Nashville, TN: Abingdon Press, 1983.

Holloway, Julian and James Kneale. "Locating Haunting: A Ghost-Hunter's Guide." *Cultural Geographies* 15, no. 3 (2008): 297–312.

Holvast, Rene. *Spiritual Mapping in the United States and Argentina, 1989–2005: Geography of Fear*. Boston: Brill, 2009.

Hunt, Stephen. "Managing the Demonic: Some Aspects of Neo-Pentecostal Deliverance Ministry." *Journal of Contemporary Religion* 13, no. 2 (1998): 215–230.

Hutchison, William R. *Religious Pluralism in America: The Contentious History of a Founding Ideal*. Hartford, CT: Yale University Press, 2004.

Illouz, Eva. *Oprah Winfrey and the Glamour of Misery: An Essay on Popular Culture*. New York: Columbia University Press, 2003.

———. *Cold Intimacies: The Making of Emotional Capitalism*. Malden, MA: Polity Press, 2007.

———. *Saving the Modern Soul: Therapy, Emotions, and the Culture of Self-Help*. Berkeley: University of California Press, 2008.

———. *Why Love Hurts*. Malden, MA: Polity Press, 2012.

Imber, Jonathan, ed. *Therapeutic Culture: Triumph and Defeat*. Piscataway, NJ: Transaction Publishers, 2004.

Ingebretson, S.J.; Edward J. *Maps of Heaven, Maps of Hell: Religious Terror as Memory from the Puritans to Stephen King*. London: M.E. Sharpe, 1996.

Ivey, Paul Eli. "Harmonialism and Metaphysical Religion." In *Encyclopedia of Religion in America*, edited by Charles H. Lippy and Peter W. Williams. Washington, DC: CQ Press, 2010.

Jacobs, Cindy. "Dealing with Strongholds." In *Breaking Strongholds in Your City: How to Use Spiritual Mapping to Make Your Prayers More Strategic, Effective and Targeted*, edited by C. Peter Wagner, 73–96. Ventura, CA: Regal Books, 1993.

———. *Possessing the Gates of the Enemy: A Training Manual for Militant Intercession*. Second edition with study guide. Grand Rapids, MI: Baker Books, 1994.

———. *The Voice of God: How God Speaks Personally and Corporately to His Children Today*. Ventura, CA: Regal Books, 1995.

———. *Deliver Us from Evil: Putting a Stop to the Occultic Influence Invading Your Home and Community*. Ventura, CA: Regal Books, 2001.

———. *The Reformation Manifesto*. Minneapolis, MN: Bethany House Publishers, 2008.

Jagel, Katie. "Poll Results: Exorcism." *Yougov: What the World Thinks*, September 17, 2013. http://today.yougov.com/news/2013/09/17/poll-results-exorcism/. Accessed June 19, 2014.

Jakobsen, Janet and Ann Pellegrini, *Love the Sin: Sexual Regulation and the Limits of Religious Tolerance*. Boston: Beacon Press, 2004.

——— and Ann Pellegrini, eds. *Secularisms*. Durham, NC: Duke University Press, 2008.

Jorgenson, Dan. "Third Wave Evangelism and the Politics of the Global in Papua New Guinea: Spiritual Warfare and the Recreation of Place in Telefolmin." *Oceania* 75 (2005): 444–461.

Kapchan, Deborah A. and Pauline Turner Strong, "Theorizing the Hybrid." *Journal of American Folklore* 112, no. 445 (Summer 1999): 239–253.

Kapferer, Bruce, Kari Telle, and Annelin Eriksen, eds. *Contemporary Religiosities: Emergent Socialities and the Post-Nation-State*. New York: Berghahn Books, 2010.

Keane, Webb. *Christian Moderns: Freedom and Fetish in the Mission Encounter*. Berkeley: The University of California Press, 2007.

Kendall, Laurel, Vu Thi Thanh Tam, and Nguyen Thi Thu Huong. "Beautiful and Efficacious Statues: Magic, Commodities, Agency, and the Production of Sacred Objects in Popular Religion in Vietnam." *Material Religion* 6, no. 1 (2010): 60–85.

Kintz, Linda. *Between Jesus and the Market: The Emotions that Matter in Right-Wing America*. Durham, NC: Duke University Press, 1997.

Kosmin, Barry, Ariela Keysar, Ryan Cragun, and Juham Navarro-Rivera. "American Nones: The Profile of the No Religion Population." Hartford, CT: Trinity College, 2009.

———, Egon Mayer, and Ariela Keysar. "American Religious Identification Survey 2001." New York: The Graduate Center of the City University of New York, 2001.

Kraft, Charles. "Response." In *Wrestling with Dark Angels: Toward a Deeper Understanding of the Supernatural Forces in Spiritual Warfare*, edited by C. Peter Wagner and F. Douglas Pennoyer, 271–279. Ventura, CA: Regal Books, 1990.

Kwilecki, Susan. "Twenty-First-Century American Ghosts: Therapy and Revelation from beyond the Grave." *Religion and American Culture* 19, no. 1 (2009): 101–133.

Lampman, Jane. "'The Secret,' a Phenomenon, is no mystery to many." *The Christian Science Monitor*, March 28, 2007. http://www. csmonitor.com/2007/0328/p13s01-lire.html. Accessed August 30, 2012.

Laycock, Joseph L. "The Folk Piety of Peter Blatty: *The Exorcist* in the Context of Secularization." *Interdisciplinary Journal of Research on*

Religion 5, Article 6 (2009). http://www.religjournal.com/articles/article_view.php?id=35. Accessed July 22, 2012.

Leopold, Anita Maria and Jeppe Sinding Jensen, eds. *Syncretism in Religion: A Reader*. New York: Routledge, 2004.

Lienesch, Michael. *Redeeming America: Piety and Politics in the New Christian Right*. Chapel Hill: The University of North Carolina Press, 1993.

Lofton, Kathryn. *Oprah: The Gospel of an Icon*. Berkeley: University of California Press, 2011.

Long, Carolyn Morrow. *Spiritual Merchants: Religion, Magic, and Commerce*. Knoxville: The University of Tennessee Press, 2001.

Luhr, Eileen. *Witnessing Suburbia: Conservatives and Christian Youth Culture*. Berkeley: University of California Press, 2009.

———. "Punk, Metal, and American Religions." *Religion Compass* 4, no. 7 (2010): 443–451

Lyons, Linda. "One-Third of Americans Believe Dearly May Not Have Departed." *Gallup*, July 12, 2005. http://www.gallup.com/poll/17275/onethird-americans-believe-dearly-may-departed.aspx. Accessed April 12, 2013.

Mantyla, Kyle. "Rick Perry, Alice Patterson, and the Demons who Control Our Politics." *Right Wing Watch* (August 12, 2011). http://www.rightwingwatch.org/content/rick-perry-alice-patterson-and-demons-who-control-our-politics. Accessed May 9, 2013.

Marsden, George. *Fundamentalism and American Culture: The Shaping of Twentieth-Century Evangelicalism, 1870–1925*. New York: Oxford University Press, 1980.

———. *Reforming Fundamentalism: Fuller Seminary and the New Evangelicalism*. Grand Rapids, MI: Eerdmans, 1987.

Martikainen, Tuomas and Francois Gauthier, eds. *Religion in a Neoliberal Age: Political Economy and Modes of Governance*. Burlington, VT: Ashgate, 2013.

Martin, David. *Pentecostalism: The World Their Parish*. Boston: Wiley-Blackwell, 2001.

Martin, William. *With God on Our Side: The Rise of the Religious Right in America*. New York: Broadway Books, 2005.

Mate, Gabor. In *the Realm of Hungry Ghosts: Close Encounters with Addiction*. Berkeley, CA: North Atlantic Books, 2010.

Maysh, Jeff. "'We're not like Normal Teenagers': Meet the Exorcist
Schoolgirls who Spend Their Time Casting Out Demons around the
World." *Daily Mail* (August 11, 2011). http://www.dailymail.co.uk/
news/article-2024621/Meet-exorcist-schoolgirls-spend-time-casting-
demons-worldwide.html. Accessed June 4, 2012.

McAlister, Elizabeth. "Globalization and the Religious Production of
Space." *Journal for the Scientific Study of Religion* 44, no. 3 (2005):
249–255.

McCloud, Sean. *Making the American Religious Fringe: Exotics,
Subversives, and Journalists, 1955–1993.* Chapel Hill: The University
of North Carolina Press, 2004.

———. *Divine Hierarchies: Class in American Religion and Religious
Studies.* Chapel Hill: The University of North Carolina Press, 2007

———. "Liminal Subjectivities and Religious Change: Circumscribing
Giddens for the Study of American Religion." *Journal of
Contemporary Religion* 22, no. 3 (October 2007): 295–309.

———. "Religion and Modern Culture." Bibliographic Essay.
CHOICE: Current Reviews for Academic Libraries (May 2007):
1439–1451.

———. "Hardcore Scholarship and High School Cliques." *Bulletin for
the Study of Religion* 41, no. 4 (November 2012): 33–36.

———. "The Possibilities of Change in a World of Constraint: Individual
and Social Transformation in the Work of Pierre Bourdieu." *Bulletin
for the Study of Religion* 41, no. 1 (2012): 2–8.

McConeghy, Dave. "Demons, Possessions, and Exorcisms: Sean McCloud
on Spiritual Warfare." *Religious Studies Project.* April 14, 2014. http://
www.religiousstudiesproject.com/podcast/sean-mccloud-on-spiritual-
warfare/. Accessed June 19, 2014:

McGarry, Molly. *Ghosts of Futures Past: Spiritualism and the Cultural
Politics of Nineteenth-Century America.* Berkeley: University of
California Press, 2008.

McGraw, Phil. *Self Matters: Creating Your Life from the Inside Out.* New
York: Free Press, 2003.

———. *Real Life: Preparing for the 7 Most Challenging Days of Your
Life.* New York: Free Press, 2009.

McGuire, Meredith. *Lived Religion: Faith and Practice in Everyday Life.*
New York: Oxford University Press, 2008.

McKinnon, Andrew. "Ideology and the Market Metaphor in Rational Choice Theory of Religion: A Rhetorical Critique of 'Religious Economies.'" *Critical Sociology* 39 (July 2013): 529–543.

Meyer, Birgit. "Pentecostalism and Neo-Liberal Capitalism: Faith, Prosperity and Vision in African Pentecostal-Charismatic Churches." *Journal for the Study of Religion* 20, no. 2 (2007): 5–28.

Miller, Daniel. *The Comfort of Things*. Malden, MA: Polity Press, 2008.

Modern, John Lardas. *Secularism in Antebellum America*. Chicago: The University of Chicago Press, 2011.

Monk, Maria. *The Awful Disclosures of Maria Monk*. London: Houlston and Stoneman, 1851.

Monteith, Andrew. "Demons, Exoticism, and the Academy." *The Religious Studies Project*. April 17, 2014. http://www.religiousstudiesproject. com/2014/04/17/demons-exoticism-and-the-academy-by-andrew-monteith/. Accessed June 19, 2014:

Moreton, Bethany. "The Soul of Neoliberalism." *Social Text* 92 25, no. 3 (Fall 2007): 104–123.

———. *To Serve God and Wal-Mart: The Making of Christian Free Enterprise*. Cambridge, MA: Harvard University Press, 2009.

Morgan, David. *Visual Piety: A History and Theory of Popular Religious Images*. Berkeley: University of California Press, 1998.

Murphy, Ed. "We are at War." In *Wrestling with Dark Angels: Toward a Deeper Understanding of the Supernatural Forces in Spiritual Warfare*, edited by C. Peter Wagner and F. Douglas Pennoyer, 49–72. Ventura, CA: Regal Books, 1990.

———. *The Handbook for Spiritual Warfare*. Revised and updated. Nashville: Thomas Nelson Publishers, 2003.

Nahi, Alon and Haim Omer. "Demonic and Tragic Narratives in Psychotherapy." In *Healing Plots: The Narrative Basis of Psychotherapy*, edited by Amia Lieblich, Dan McAdams, and Ruthellen Josselson, 29–48. Washington, DC: American Psychological Association, 2004.

Neal, Lynn S. "Christianizing the Klan: Alma White, Branford Clarke, and the Art of Religious Intolerance." *Church History* 78, no. 2 (June 2009): 350–378.

New Apostolic Reformation Research Team. "Spiritual Mapping and Spiritual Warfare—Muthee and the 'Transformations' Franchise." *Talk*

to Action, October 30, 2008. http://www.talk2action.org/story/2008/
10/27/115813/98. Accessed July 23, 2012.

O' Neill, Kevin Lewis. *City of God: Christian Citizenship in Postwar
Guatemala.* Berkeley: University of California Press, 2010.

Osteen, Joel. *Your Best Life Now: 7 Steps to Living at Your Full
Potential.* New York: Faithwords, 2004.

Ostling, Richard N. "The Church Search." *Time* 141, no. 14 (April 5,
1993): 44–49.

Otis Jr., George. *Informed Intercession.* Ventura: Renew Books, 1999.

———, director. *The Quickening: Entering into the Firestorm of God's
Grace.* Transformations Media, 2003.

Palmisano, Stefania. "New Monasticism and the Consumer Economy: A
Paradox?" Paper Presentation at SOCREL Study Group of the British
Sociological Association. March 2012.

Patterson, Alice. *Bridging the Racial and Political Divide: How Godly
Politics Can Transform a Nation.* San Jose, CA: Transformational
Publications—A Division of Harvest Evangelism, 2010.

Peale, Norman Vincent. *The Power of Positive Thinking.* New York:
Simon and Schuster, 1952.

Peck, M. Scott. *The Road Less Travelled: A New Psychology of Love,
Traditional Values and Spiritual Growth.* New York: Simon and
Schuster, 1978.

Peck, Janice. "Psychologized Religion in a Mediated World." In
Rethinking Media, Religion, and Culture, edited by Stewart M.
Hoover and Knut Lundby, 227–245. Thousand Oaks, CA: Sage
Publications, 1997.

———. *The Age of Oprah: Cultural Icon for the Neoliberal Era.* Boulder,
CO: Paradigm Publishers, 2008.

Pels, Peter. "The Modern Fear of Matter: Reflections on the Protestantism
of Victorian Science." *Material Religion* 4, no. 3 (2008): 264–283.

Pennoyer, F. Douglas. "In Dark Dungeons of Collective Captivity." In
*Wrestling with Dark Angels: Toward a Deeper Understanding of
the Supernatural Forces in Spiritual Warfare,* edited by C. Peter
Wagner and F. Douglas Pennoyer, 249–270. Ventura, CA: Regal
Books, 1990.

Percy, Jennifer. *Demon Camp: A Soldier's Exorcism.* New York:
Scribner's, 2014.

Pew Research Center. "Many Americans Mix Multiple Faiths." np: Pew Forum on Religion and Public Life, 2009.

———. "U.S. Religious Landscape Survey." http://pewresearch.org/databank/dailynumber/?NumberID=885. Accessed September 1, 2012.

Pierce, Chuck D. and Rebecca Wagner Systema. *Protecting Your Home from Spiritual Darkness*. Ventura, CA: Regal Books, 2004.

Pierce, Charles. "It Has Come to This: Hot Teen Exorcists." *Esquire Politics Blog,* April 5, 2012. http://www.esquire.com/blogs/politics/teen-exorcists-7865947. Accessed July 13, 2012.

Pike, Sarah. "Dark Teens and Born-Again Martyrs: Captivity Narratives after Columbine." *Journal of the American Academy of Religion* 77, no. 3 (2009): 647–679.

Poole, W. Scott. *Satan in America: The Devil We Know*. Lanham, MD: Rowan and Littlefield, 2010.

———. *Monsters in America: Our Historical Obsession with the Hideous and the Haunting*. Waco, TX: Baylor University Press, 2011.

Powlison, David. "Response to C. Peter Wagner and Rebecca Greenwood." In *Understanding Spiritual Warfare: Four Views*, edited by James K. Beilby and Paul Rhodes Eddy, 204–209. Grand Rapids, MI: Baker Academic, 2012.

Pratt, Thomas. "The Need to Dialogue: A Review of the Debate on the Controversy of Signs, Wonders, Miracles, and Spiritual Warfare Raised in the Literature of the Third Wave Movement." *Pneuma: The Journal of the Society of Pentecostal Studies* 13, no. 1 (1991): 7–32.

Prothero, Stephen. *American Jesus: How the Son of God Became a National Icon*. New York: Farrar, Straus, and Giroux, 2003.

——— (ed). *A Nation of Religions: The Politics of Pluralism in Multireligious America*. Chapel Hill: The University of North Carolina Press, 2006.

Putnam, Robert D. and David E. Campbell. *American Grace: How Religion Divides and Unites Us*. New York: Simon and Schuster, 2010.

Rehfeld, Nina. "Sie wollen unsere Seelen retten: Diese Teenager treiben uns den Teufel aus." *Glamour* (German edition), May 2012: 236–239.

Relph, E.C. *Place and Placelessness*. London: Pion, 1976.

Richardson, Judith. *Possessions: The History and Uses of Haunting in the Hudson Valley*. Cambridge, MA: Harvard University Press, 2003.

Richardson James T., Joel Best, and David G. Bromley, eds. *The Satanism Scare*. New York: Aldine De Gruyter, 1991.

Rief, Phillip. *Triumph of the Therapeutic: Uses of Faith after Freud*. New York: Harper and Row, 1966.

Robbins, Joel. "Crypto-Religion and the Study of Cultural Mixes: Anthropology, Value, and the Nature of Syncretism." *Journal of the American Academy of Religion* 79, no. 2 (June 2011): 408–424.

Rodgers, Daniel T. *Age of Fracture*. Cambridge, MA: Belknap/Harvard University Press, 2011.

Roof, Wade Clark. *Spiritual Marketplace: Baby Boomers and the Remaking of American Religion*. Princeton, NJ: Princeton University Press, 1999.

——— and William McKinney, *American Mainline Religion: Its Changing Shape and Future*. New Brunswick, NJ: Rutgers University Press, 1987.

Rose, Tom. *Economics: Principles and Policies from a Christian Perspective*. Mercer, PA: American Enterprise Publications, 1986.

Roy, Olivier. *Holy Ignorance: When Religion and Culture Part Ways*. New York: Columbia University Press, 2010.

Russell, Cheryl. *The Master Trend: How the Baby Boom Generation Is Remaking America*. New York: Perseus, 1993.

Saad-Filho, Alfredo and Deborah Johnston, eds. *Neoliberalism: A Critical Reader*. London: Pluto Press, 2005.

Sanders, Todd. "Buses in Bongoland: Seductive Analytics and the Occult." *Anthropological Theory* 8, no. 2 (2008): 107–132.

Sargeant, Kimon Howland. *Seeker Churches: Promoting Traditional Religion in a Nontraditional Way*. Piscataway, NJ: Rutgers University Press, 2000.

Satter, Beryl. *Each Mind a Kingdom: American Women, Sexual Purity, and the New Thought Movement, 1875–1920*. Berkeley: University of California Press, 2001.

Schmidt, Leigh. *Hearing Things: Religion, Illusion, and the American Enlightenment*. Cambridge, MA: Harvard University Press, 2000.

Sconce, Jeffrey. *Haunted Media: Electronic Presence from Telegraphy to Television*. Durham, NC: Duke University Press, 2000.

Sennett, Richard. *The Corrosion of Character: The Personal Consequences of Work in the New Capitalism*. New York: W.W. Norton and Company, 2000.

———. *The Culture of the New Capitalism*. New Haven, CT: Yale University Press, 2006.

Shaw, Rosiland and Charles Stewart, eds. *Syncretism/Anti-Syncretism: The Politics of Religious Synthesis*. New York: Routledge, 1994.

Silvoso, Edward. *Anointed for Business: How to Use Your Influence in the Marketplace to Change the World*. Ventura, CA: Regal Books, 2002.

———. *Transformation: Change the Marketplace and You Change the World*. Ventura, CA: Regal Books, 2010.

Sjoberg, Kjell. "Spiritual Mapping for Prophetic Prayer Actions." In *Breaking Strongholds in Your City: How to use Spiritual Mapping to Make Your Prayers More Strategic, Effective and Targeted*, edited by C. Peter Wagner, 97–119. Ventura, CA: Regal Books, 1993.

Smith, Eddie. *Breaking the Enemy's Grip*. Minneapolis, MN: Bethany House Publishers, 2004.

Smith, Alice. *Beyond the Lie: Finding Freedom from the Past*. Minneapolis, MN: Bethany House Publishers, 2006.

Smith, Jacob. "Turn Me On, Dead Media: A Backward Look at the Re-Enchantment of an Old Medium." *Television and New Media* 12, no. 6 (2011): 531–551.

Smith, Eddie and Alice Smith. *Spiritual Housecleaning: Protect Your Home and Family From Spiritual Pollution*. Ventura, CA: Regal Books, 2003.

———. *Spiritual Housecleaning Workbook: Amazing Stories and Practical Steps on How to Protect Your Home and Family from Spiritual Pollution*. Ventura, CA: Regal Books, 2007.

Spooner, Catherine and Emma McEvoy, "Introduction." In *The Routledge Companion to Gothic*, edited by Catherine Spooner and Emma McEvoy, 1–4. New York: Routledge, 2007.

Stark, Rodney and Roger Finke. *Acts of Faith: Explaining the Human Side of Religion*. Berkeley: University of California Press, 2000.

Stephens, Walter. *Demon Lovers: Witchcraft, Sex, and the Crisis of Belief*. Chicago: The University of Chicago Press, 2002.

Stewart, Charles. "Syncretism and Its Synonyms: Reflections on Cultural Mixture." *Diacritics* 29, no. 3 (Fall 1999): 40–62.

Stoker, Bram. *Dracula*. Norton Critical Edition, edited by Nina Auerbach and David J. Skal. New York: W. W. Norton & Company, 1996.

Stone, Perry. *Purging Your Family Tree: How to Rid Your Home and Family of Demonic Influence and Generational Oppression*. Lake Mary, FL: Charisma House, 2011.

Stowe, David W. *No Sympathy for the Devil: Christian Pop Music and the Transformation of American Evangelicalism*. Chapel Hill: The University of North Carolina Press, 2011.

Sullivan, Winnifred. *The Impossibility of Religious Freedom*. Princeton, NJ: Princeton University Press, 2007.

Swidler, Ann. *Talk of Love: How Culture Matters*. Chicago: University of Chicago Press, 2001.

Tamney, Joseph. *The Resilience of Conservative Religion: The Case of Popular, Conservative Congregations*. New York: Cambridge University Press, 2002.

Taylor, Humphrey. "The Religious and Other Beliefs of Americans 2003." Rochester, NY: Harris Interactive, 2003.

Taylor, Charles. *A Secular Age*. Cambridge, MA: Belknap/Harvard University Press, 2007.

Tuan, Yi Fu. *Space and Place: The Perspective of Experience*. Minneapolis: The University of Minnesota Press, 1977.

———. *Topophilia: A Study of Environmental Perception, Values, and Attitudes*. New York: Columbia University Press, 1990.

Turkle, Sherry. *Alone Together: Why We Expect More from Technology and Less from Each Other*. New York: Basic Books, 2011.

Tweed, Thomas A. "Introduction: Narrating U.S. Religious History." In *Retelling U.S. Religious History*, edited by Thomas A. Tweed, 1–24. Berkeley: University of California Press, 1997.

Twiss, Richard. *One Church, Many Tribes: Following Jesus the Way God Made You*. Ventura, CA: Regal Books, 2003.

Urban, Hugh. "Avatar for Our Age: Sathya Sai Baba and the Cultural Contradictions of Late Capitalism." *Religion* 33 (2003): 73–93.

Victor, Jeffrey. *Satanic Panic: The Creation of a Contemporary Legend*. Chicago: Open Court Press, 1993.

Voskuil, Dennis. *Mountains into Goldmines: Robert Schuller and the Gospel of Success*. Grand Rapids, MI: Eerdmans, 1983.

Wacker, Grant. "Pentecostalism." In *The Encyclopedia of the American Religious Experience*, edited by Charles Lippy and Peter Williams, 933–945. New York: Scribners, 1988.

———. *Heaven Below: Early Pentecostals and American Culture.* Cambridge, MA: Harvard University Press, 2003.

Wagner, C. Peter. "The Third Wave." *Christian Life* (September 1984): np.

———. *The Third Wave of the Holy Spirit: Encountering the Power of Signs and Wonders.* Ann Arbor, MI: Vine Books, 1988.

———. "Territorial Spirits." In *Wrestling with Dark Angels: Toward a Deeper Understanding of the Supernatural Forces in Spiritual Warfare*, edited by C. Peter Wagner and F. Douglas Pennoyer, 73–91. Ventura, CA: Regal Books, 1990.

———. *Warfare Prayer: How to Seek God's Power and Protection in the Battle to Build His Kingdom.* Ventura, CA: Regal Books, 1992.

———, ed. *Breaking Strongholds in Your City: How to Use Spiritual Mapping to Make Your Prayers More Strategic, Effective and Targeted.* Ventura, CA: Regal Books, 1993.

———. "The Visible and the Invisible." In *Breaking Strongholds in Your City: How to Use Spiritual Mapping to Make Your Prayers More Strategic, Effective and Targeted*, edited by C. Peter Wagner, 49–72. Ventura, CA: Regal Books, 1993.

———. *Confronting the Queen of Heaven.* Pasadena, CA: Wagner Institute Publications, 2001.

——— and F. Douglas Pennoyer, eds. *Wrestling with Dark Angels: Toward a Deeper Understanding of the Supernatural Forces in Spiritual Warfare.* Ventura, CA: Regal Books, 1990.

Warner, Maria. *Phantasmagoria: Spirit Visions, Metaphors, and Media into the Twenty-first Century.* New York: Oxford University Press, 2006.

Warren, Rick. *The Purpose Driven Life.* Grand Rapids, MI: Zondervan, 2002.

Warren, Rick. *The Purpose-Driven Life Journal.* Grand Rapids, MI: Zondervan, 2002.

Watts, Jill. *God, Harlem USA: The Father Divine Story.* Berkeley: University of California Press, 1995.

Weaver, John. "Upardonable Sins: The Mentally Ill and Evangelicalism in America." *The Journal of Religion and Popular Culture* 23, no. 1 (April 2011): 65–81.

Weber, Max. "The Social Psychology of the World's Religions." In *From Max Weber: Essays in Sociology*, edited by H. H. Gerth and C. Wright Mills, 267–301. New York: Oxford University Press, 1946.

Weiner, Isaac. "Sound and American Religions." *Religion Compass* 3, no. 5 (2009): 897–908.

Weinstock, Jeffrey. "Introduction: The Spectral Turn." In *Spectral America: Phantoms and the National Imagination*, edited by Jeffrey Weinstock, 3–17. Madison: University of Wisconsin Press, 2004.

White, Alma. *Demons and Tongues*. Zarephath, NJ: Pillar of Fire Publishers, 1949.

Whitehead, Amy. "The Goddess and the Virgin: Materiality in Western Europe." *The Pomegranate* 10, no. 2 (2008): 163–183.

Wilson, Bruce. "Palin's Churches and the New Apostolic Reformation." *Talk to Action,* September 5, 2008. http://www.talk2action.org/story/2008/9/5/114652/6239. Accessed July 23, 2012.

Wink, Walter and Michael Hardin, "Response to C. Peter Wagner and Rebecca Greenwood." In *Understanding Spiritual Warfare: Four Views*, edited by James K. Beilby and Paul Rhodes Eddy, 199–203. Grand Rapids, MI: Baker Academic, 2012.

Wood, Matthew. "Capital Possession: A Comparative Approach to 'New Age' Control of the Means of Possession." *Culture and Religion* 4, no. 1 (2003): 159–182.

———. *Possession, Power, and the New Age: Ambiguities of Authority in Neoliberal Societies*. Burlington, VT: Ashgate, 2007.

Wuthnow, Robert. *The Restructuring of American Religion*. Princeton, NJ: Princeton University Press, 1988.

———. *After Heaven: Spirituality in America Since the 1950s*. Berkeley: University of California Press, 1998.

Yamane, David. "Secularization on Trial: In Defense of a Neo-Secularization Paradigm." *Journal for the Scientific Study of Religion* 36, no. 2 (1997): 107–120.

INDEX